BRAVERY BECOMES YOU
On the Road to Fearless and Free

We all strive to be brave, as we face life's inevitable losses and challenges — on every page of Bravery Becomes You, *Sandy Travis Bildahl leads us closer to our deepest well of courage and strength.*

IRIS KRASNOW, *New York Times*-bestselling author

Facing fear has never been so much fun and life-changing. Sandy's self-reflective book is a page-turner! You don't want to miss it. With her engaging writing style, Sandy takes you on the road to discover, as she did, a new mindset that answers the question, "What would I do if I were brave?" And then do it! As Sandy says, "The risk is in not taking the risk." Don't risk missing this book!

SHELLEY ROW, PE, CSP, author of
Think Less Live More: Lessons from a Recovering Over-Thinker
Named by *Inc. Magazine* as one of the top 100 leadership speakers

Do you want to feel more joy, aliveness, and fun in your life? Then read this book. Sandy shares the secret to satisfied, contented happiness. And the key....bravery. But Sandy doesn't just tell you how to be brave and leave it at that. No, she shows you... through her own journey of self-discovery...all the while taking you along for the adventure of a lifetime. In Sandy's own words, "Imagine the power of YOU as you let go of fear's interference, build unstoppable confidence, and make a passionate commitment to being true to yourself and the future you want." YES! This fun, thought-provoking, and inspiring book will help you get there.

LIZ FLETCHER BROWN, author of the award-winning book
Full Wattage! A Practical Guide to Living a Purposeful Life Worth Celebrating

A gifted writer and storyteller, Sandy Travis Bildahl artfully blends her humor, insights, and wisdom and takes us on a wild journey with her son Travis to transcend crippling fear and reclaim her true power. Neuroscience tells us that when Bravery "literally" Becomes You, you're no longer neurologically, neurochemically, or emotionally tethered to old, hardwired ways of thinking, behaving, and feeling. When you get beyond the old thought/feeling fear loop and choose to step into the unknown – despite the discomfort – you turn your fear into passion and courage. How do you make that shift? Sandy shows us the way with her simple, yet powerful guide to creating an exquisite life, filled with greater freedom, wholeness, adventure, and self love.

KARIN SOKEL, *NeuroChange Solutions* Consultant

Sandy Travis Bildahl has written an engaging and thought-provoking book! From the beginning, the reader is introduced to the author's self-reflective style as she shares her resistance and doubts about accepting her son's invitation to join him on a six-week camping road trip. Saying "yes" to herself as much as to her son, they embark on a once-in-a-lifetime trip. She details their adventure through storytelling and sharing her very honest personal inner dialogue making the experience completely relatable. As Sandy's revelations surface on her transformative journey she invites readers to consider their own fears and encourages them to move bravely forward with a practical guide of thoughtful prompts woven within the chapters. If you're ready to make a shift in your life accompanied by a trustworthy companion who has walked her talk, I highly recommend this book.

GILLIAN STEVENS, author of
the Amazon Bestseller and Canada Book Award winner
*Explore, Transform, Flourish - Support and Hope for Those Who Help Others:
How Professionals Keep It Together* and *Your SELF Guided Journal to
Health, Happiness, and Getting What You Want*

BRAVERY
BECOMES
On the Road to Fearless and Free
YOU

SANDY TRAVIS BILDAHL

Worthwords Publishing

Annapolis, MD

worthwordspublishing@gmail.com

Library of Congress Control Number: 2021907362

First paperback edition April 2021
Book design by Peri Gabriel Design

Worthwords Publishing

1783 Forest Drive
Annapolis, MD 21401
www.worthwordspublishing.com

Book: ISBN 978-1-7366851-0-5
Ebook: ISBN 978-1-7366851-1-2

For my mother,

who always told me

that anything is possible

if you're brave enough to take a chance

and follow your dreams.

Our Journey

Contents

"Are we going to die?

As the tires edged over the crumbling white line,

the car tipping over the ragged rocks,

I wondered how many had driven over this same cliff.

Would we be next?"

>>‹◌›»

Foreword

THE MORE WE STEP OUT of the familiar, the easier it becomes to let go of the ties that bind us to our ordinary, safe lives. When we learn how to recognize our fear patterns, we begin to question their truth, let go of the obstacles they create and discover the best life lesson of all. Happiness awaits you on the other side.

I met Sandy about a decade ago. We were part of, and still belong to, a group of women who joined together to become conscious creators of living our best lives. Unbeknownst to us, we were entering what she calls the brave zone.

I know a little something about bravery. I bet you do too. Shortly before I met Sandy, I was embarking on my own heroine's journey. I was gearing up to hike the Appalachian Trail. It meant that I had to learn about backpacking and how to navigate the daily life of being a backpacker. It was daunting!

But, like the heroine's journey, a meaningful outcome is achieved when bravery overrides fear, one step at a time. It requires a new set of thinking skills and a mindset reset. For me, small accomplishments led to significant achievements. Bravery builds confidence. Confidence gives us happiness. As Sandy says, "Personal bravery isn't about running into a burning building to save lives, it's about standing up for who you are and who you want to be and enjoying life on your terms. Big steps or small, it's up to you."

Sandy and I have formed a tight friendship. When she first told me about her idea – *Bravery Becomes You* – I was intrigued! Over the past few years, I watched her dreams unfold. She is a woman who walks her talk and does it with great humor and depth of perception. I do not doubt that you will see and experience this as you read this book. She has been a mentor to me and has coached and presented her fear navigation system to many. Sandy has given me a new life mantra —"How will I feel if I do? How will I feel if I don't?" It works! Her entertaining yet powerful story of transformation can change your life, as it has changed mine. It begins with turning this page.

SHERRY ROGERS
Writer, Photographer, and Storyteller at Echoes in the Wild

Preface

You're Invited

To a New Way of Living
Brave, Confident, and Content

DEAR READER,

DO YOU EVER HEAR THAT quiet, persistent voice that says, "Don't you think it's time to do what you *really* want to do?" I know that voice well. And once I crossed the threshold of 50 and now 60, that inner voice seemed louder, more urgent. My response? "I'll get back to you." Why? No time. Too busy. Overwhelmed. Clearly, I wasn't ready to face what I wanted to do and the work it would take. On most levels, my life seemed fine. I was proud of my accomplishments. But who was I kidding? Something wasn't right. Slowly the message began to sink in. And questions like, "What's missing? What's next?" and "Why do I feel so restless?" had no answers. I was stuck.

So there I stood at the crossroads of bloom or fade knowing that I wasn't done growing, having fun, or wanting my life to have meaning, purpose, and a sense of adventure. And I knew I'd better do something about it soon because...reality check...time was no longer on my side. I had arrived at a new stage of life where my old reliable answers about who I am weren't resonating. And yet, I couldn't figure out what to do about it.

I wasn't alone. Everywhere I went with old and new friends, at work with my coaching clients, and in the many books I read, lots of people were feeling the same thing. You too?

So what is this?

It's an out-of-sync, confusing, soul-searching, questioning, "Who do I want to be?" and "What do I want to do?" time of life. And even more discouraging? "Why aren't all our 'life smarts' stepping up with answers?"

We can feel the pulse of the future knocking. Every moment brimming with possibility. And yet it can feel like standing on the edge of a high dive, toes curled over the board's edge, unsure whether to jump. Yes? No? Yes? No? Yes? Leap into what, exactly?

Whatever you want!

Because you're right on time. Poised for life's next great chapter. The fact that you are inquiring, curious, and simply want more meaning, purpose, and joy every day means that your inner intelligence has been activated. You're ready to embrace a new way of thinking about YOU.

And the good news? The pro-age era (versus anti-aging) has arrived. Which means the world is more open and ready to be inspired by whatever you choose to be and do.

So how do you start this exciting new journey? First, you need to consider why your future's been hanging out at the bottom of your to-do list. The answer?

FEAR.

Fear because we're no longer sure exactly what we want. Fear that maybe we don't have the energy or ability to try something new. Fear that we're being phased out of the business market. Fear of being alone. Fear that our old notion of strong and capable may no longer apply. Fear because the face in the mirror is changing. And a big one? We're afraid we're running out of time!

Worst of all, we're going about everything the long way and frankly the wrong way - the old way, which means we're relying on a mindset that's expired! The energy of the past was about finding the right career, the right husband or partner, the right house, the right schools for children, the right vacations, enough money to make it all happen and at least be comfortable...and on and on. But now, meeting the world's expectations is no longer inspiring and society doesn't offer a path forward except, "It's time to retire, sit back and relax. Enjoy doing nothing." How exciting is that?

Those options were a wake-up call for me. I was responsible for creating my future! Could I let go of the past, surrender to the unknown, and believe I had the power to actually change, based on what I wanted more than anything? It was up to me.

So with fear hanging around, how did I do that? *Bravery Becomes You* to the rescue - the new mindset I discovered that's a perfect match for this new way of living. More than anything, I wanted to wake up in the morning excited, clear, and focused on what was most important to me.

And that didn't mean ignoring or losing the people I love or tossing aside all the details of my past. It meant creating an unwavering commitment to inquire, uncover, activate and enjoy myself doing whatever I choose to do starting now. Imagine! A new future that resonates with me!!!

What I now live and love is a process of discovery, the habit of standing up for who you *really* are, who you want to be, and making one thing clear: fear isn't going to stop you. It won't. It can't. It doesn't have a chance.

So are you ready to wake up happy, inspired, and brave? Yes!

But...

Can you feel yourself wavering? Ready..but..but...

Nice idea, right? But wait; let's be realistic. What do you do with the unexpected life challenges that show up just as you're ready to focus on you? I know from my clients and my own experience, that creating and living a vibrant new vision of the future (that we all long for) is also happening in the midst of wrestling with a variety of issues we never thought we'd face.

I like to think of them as detours (not stop signs). Here are some examples:

Divorce. Death of a spouse. Retirement. Money troubles. Caretaking. You want/need a new job? And I can't omit...Aging. All these situations are normal, but they all require a shift in expectations.

So how do you thrive when so many things ask for your attention? How do you create the adventure of Future You?

All journeys have obstacles and challenges, and yours will too. But the truth is that problems are often fuel for your growth, empathy, and understanding. Hardships are an opportunity to strengthen your brave self. What's the point of bravery if you have nothing to fear?

That was the question I answered when a *Bravery Becomes You* opportunity showed up. My 24-year-old son invited me on a six-week camping road trip. That's not what I was hoping for. I didn't want it. It certainly wasn't on my wishlist. But after a lot of mental negotiation, I said YES and discovered exactly what I needed to test the principles of *Bravery Becomes You*. It was time to walk the talk.

That YES turned into a gift of time and space. I was able to step away from my day-to-day routine and experience who I am in a setting where I had no preconceived ideas of how it would be. This six-week "free zone" made it possible to examine my fears and test the fearless self I'd always hoped would arrive and save me from all the reasons I've found to hold back and not be as strong as my inner self knew I could be.

The result? The secret to satisfied, contented happiness. I found what I'd been looking for by becoming my own bravery experiment. Today I know, without question, that nothing activates and ensures your dreams like bravery. Nothing feels better than being brave.

And now I can't wait to share everything I've learned with you. I'm inspired to help you in any way I can because I know what's possible and how good it feels. I believe with all my heart that bravery will transform your inner struggle with fear and inaction by empowering you to trust and honor yourself like never before.

On the following pages, I've recreated my road trip to include you! Together we'll travel the roads of Oregon, Washington, California, Nevada, Utah, and Colorado as I wake up to the fact that I'm scared of a lot of things and that every option in my life includes a "downside" that creates worry. What I learned? Fear was stealing my time, energy, and opportunity to enjoy every minute of my life. I had a fear story running in the background of everything I did.

But I don't want to tell you how to be brave. I want to share my adventure with you so that you can experience bravery for yourself. There are places in the book for you to stop and consider your relationship with fear and being brave. And to make your journey a success, I suggest you create your own "bravery" journal where you can write down your answers, insights and ideas. Consider it your personal inner travel log!

Bravery is also often misunderstood. So in case you think bravery is about heroic action, I want you to know that bravery isn't about big, giant accomplishments, but a simple shift in mindset that starts step by step, day by day, and keeps growing. I want you to know that nothing feels better than being brave. And once you discover the power and joy of living brave, you'll wonder why no one told you that bravery is the number one answer to living a satisfying, happy life.

So now it's time! Imagine the power of YOU as you let go of fear's interference, build unstoppable confidence that lasts, and make a passionate commitment to being true to yourself and the future you want.

YOUR FRIEND ON THE ROAD,

Sandy

PART 1

The Adventure Begins!

I'M SO GLAD YOU'RE JOINING ME. There's no time to waste. (You know why!!!) So let's get started because it's time to answer your own call to action. First step? Listen to that quiet voice within that's asking, "Who do you *really* want to be? What do you *really* want to do?" Here is where a new vision of the future begins.

And now, here's how my brave journey began for me. Here's a clue: I was listening to the wrong advice.

1

Can You Hear Me? Answer the Call

The Big YES!

SAYING YES TO MY OWN *Bravery Becomes You* adventure wasn't easy. My inner voice was calling with ideas about "what's next," while my everyday voice was giving me bad advice with its, "Get real, life is okay 'AS IS'" chant. And so, I kept hanging up. Until one day, I realized it was me calling. Me wanting the best for me. And then, I tried something new and listened in a different way. I tuned into my feelings, and heard clearly: "It's time! What are you waiting for? If not now, when?" I got it. Message received. I finally talked to ME.

Of course, that's when I got the phone call from my 24-year-old son, asking if I'd like to go on a six-week camping road trip out west. Easy answer. NO.

What?

Hmmm. Camping. Outdoors. Bears. Snakes. And the lifestyle of my son, which might not jibe with mine. And the biggest issue? I HAVE NEVER CAMPED IN MY LIFE! What kind of test was this?

Should I go? I quizzed everyone for opinions. My listening was on overdrive. Messages came from everywhere. I heard: Too uncomfortable. Too inconvenient (no showers, internet, or bathrooms). Too much time. You're too old (didn't like that one). And on and on...which led to the final agreement by most. DON'T GO! And I listened.

I remember standing in my living room shouting to the walls, "I DO NOT WANT TO GO CAMPING!!!"

But the universe was not giving up on me. Luckily, I also heard the words of the amazing young woman who cuts my hair. As I shared the pitfalls of my possible journey, she answered, "Sounds wonderful...Hope I can do that someday" and "Nothing to be afraid of."

Afraid? Me? Scared? Yes!!! But overriding that fear was her enthusiasm and words. I wanted to be like her. I wanted to be excited. I wanted to be brave.

Adding to that was the fact that my coaching business focused on the *Bravery Becomes You* concept that I had created, developed, and believed in. I'd been talking the talk...so was now the time to put words into action?

I was definitely scared, so I called in my superior powers of rationalization that said, "Hey, this fits perfectly with your general state of confusion, your longing for adventure and hey, it's also a fit with your business goals... Why not consider this 'the ultimate business trip?' Finally, something sensible and practical.

And that's when I called my son Travis and said, "YES, I'm on my way. I'm putting bravery into action."

One call. One step over the edge. Fearless here I come!

For the next six weeks, challenge and bravery were by my side, every minute!

Afraid to walk over the top of a waterfall? YES, but I pushed myself and found a way (that I thought was safe). Crawl across slippery rocks, covered with bees, and then get into a freezing cold swimming hole? YES. Awkward and uncomfortable didn't stop me as I chanted *Bravery Becomes You* and slid into the water.

Driving more than I ever thought possible through Oregon, Washington, California, Nevada, Utah, and Colorado on steep, winding roads that sometimes made me cry (or get out of the car and walk). Camping mostly on public lands and in national forests with no one in sight. (Drive down a road, pick a spot, pitch the tent.) Did I mention that we had no set itinerary?

How about days of no showers, no internet, no makeup, no bathrooms, no phone service, nobody around except bears and owls and things that rustle the trees in the night?

I resisted constantly. Did it matter if we drove 11 hours through the mountains to hear a band in a bar? Did it matter that I hadn't washed my clothes or my hair for over a week? Did it matter that we drank out of the same water bottle that was probably full of germs?

And yet? It all worked out perfectly. Every moment was 100% amazing (even the frightening uncomfortable parts). And all the worry? What was I thinking?

THINKING! It turns out that whether I'm on a great road trip or at home at my desk, the quality of my day is all about what I am thinking and how I am reacting. I knew this, but my trip added a new dimension and option to making choices that upgrade every experience. Why? I discovered how to think with my feelings first. I was learning how to navigate my life from the inside out. And being brave? It's the secret push that transforms old thinking patterns into new ones. Bravery brings the magic power and energy of adventure into everything you do. Bravery is about feeling the joy of positive energy and understanding your fears and obstacles. Getting past what holds you back feels so great that you want to do it again and again. And the more you're brave, the more confident you become. Nothing feels better—or looks better than that. And that is what *Bravery Becomes You* is all about.

I wanted to enjoy the adventure of everything a new chapter of life could offer. And it finally showed up with a little help from the ME who was waiting to be heard. I hadn't been listening to my brave voice. Now I know better.

The direction of your future is up to you and how you feel, react and listen! You're the driver behind the wheel, and you've got the map!

GETTING BRAVER—WHAT I LEARNED ABOUT FEAR: *Fearful thinking and reacting override the sound of your own voice calling. But being brave enough to listen in a new way and follow what you hear is exhilarating.*

Your listening needs a tune-up! It's time to hear the beautiful sound of your inner intelligence that's been patiently waiting to share the answers to "what should I do and how can I do it?" that you've been longing to know.

Of course, what you're hearing is the voice of your inner knowing. It often speaks quietly, sometimes it whispers, which means it's not always easy to hear. But if you listen carefully, the gentle words that are trying to guide you into a new way of being will come through loud and clear.

It's also possible you can't hear that voice. Been a while since you've checked in with yourself? A busy life can make paying attention to you seem indulgent or self-centered. But still. You know that you don't want to live every day stuck on repeat. It's kind of like reading the same book over and over again. It's time for a new chapter.

So whatever the state of your listening skills, why not turn up the volume and start a conversation with the real you that knows what feels right and what doesn't. It's reassuring to hear a voice that ignites your future direction with clarity.

That inner intelligence is also in touch with a great idea generator. Your imagination! Creative thinking, curiosity, and wonder are practical skills that offer new ideas and solutions. Creativity also instantly bypasses the grip of those familiar but rigid old ways of thinking and opens the door to exciting possibilities.

It's like waking up from years of sleep that had you believing that your dreams aren't practical and probably won't happen. But activate your imagination and discover the power of your mind to start making your ideas come alive. When a thought begins to take form, it's in the first stage of becoming real. And that's all you need to set the wheels of action into motion.

Your imagination can come up with ideas big and small, but no matter the size, the seed of your thought will grow. How big, small, wild or calm is up to you. I always say, "The size of your dreams is only limited by how big you can dream." So if you want to write a book, make it bigger. Dream success on the bestseller list. How about you're the top seller of all time. Why not? And if smaller dreams are better for you? Then do that. Unrestricted joy is yours to enjoy! There are no rules. Have fun!

Your Turn

TIME FOR YOU! From now on, each story is followed by *"bravery tools"* that will jump-start your adventure to the future. Right now we're starting with *Brave Tool #1: View from the Scenic Overlook*. There are four more that I add one-by-one following the next few stories. That's how I discovered them on my own trip, but once our journey is on a roll, you'll see all five at every stop.

AND HERE we are! Time to activate your unique vision of the future by using *Brave Tool #1: View from the Scenic Overlook*. Instructions follow.

STOP #1

VIEW *from the* SCENIC OVERLOOK

THE SCENIC OVERLOOK is where you'll preview, practice, and experience seeing your future like it's really happening! To begin, relax. Read the following. Then close your eyes and let your mind travel:

Imagine a day in the future. Go there in your imagination. See yourself. You're taking a moment to look back in time. You can see that you answered the call to be who you were longing to be, doing what you wanted to do. And it happened! You can feel it like you're there. You've never felt as good or so proud of yourself. You stood up to obstacles, let go of what no longer worked for you. You were brave! Nothing stopped you. (It doesn't matter if you know what you want right now, the goal is to activate how you want to feel, no matter what you do. Can you awaken a sense of satisfaction and joy and see yourself happy?) Now note sensations, smells, tastes, the feel of the air, sounds? Consider what you look like? What are you wearing? Is anyone there with you? Daydream the best day ever. Again, feel it like it's real. Listen to the voice within.

Then open your eyes. What did you experience? What did you do when you were brave? How did it feel? What's calling? What does the voice within say?

This is a good time to write down your thoughts. (The impact of journaling can be found in the *Three Brave Tools* section at the end of the back of the book.)

Congratulations!

You've just activated your future!

NOTE TO YOU:

VIEW FROM THE SCENIC OVERLOOK is a tool I use all the time. Imagining the future (with feeling) elevates mood, ignites purpose (being brave and standing up for who you want to be and what you want to do), and fuels motivation. It's also a great way to start the day. When I wake up and my busy mind starts whirring with my "to-do list" and worry, a moment to check in with my vision instantly turns anxiety into joy and reminds me that what I focus on is up to me.

And bonus! The more you check in with your future vision, the more it becomes real. In fact, it eventually becomes your own *Get Brave Map.* An in depth description of this tool can be found in *Three Brave Tools* at the back of the book.

Also, in case you're curious! The name of the other 4 tools, soon to be revealed, are *Shift Gears, Emergency Brake, Compass Check-In* and *Brave Travel Tip.*

NEXT:
Here's what happened when I said my first joyful YES.

2

He Hung Up the Phone

A Shaky YES

HE HUNG UP ON ME. Really? Is that how you treat your mother? Travis was ruining my joy. I was so happy about my yes. I hadn't been this excited in a long time. I felt like I was bursting with confidence (even though I hadn't done anything yet). Just deciding to move forward was activating. I loved the energy of that first yes, and I'm still feeling it today. I was so proud of myself. But at that moment I was "first-step giddy" and exuberant even though I had no idea what I had just signed up for. I'd never been camping in my life. It was true! What did I know? (I can also still remember the feeling of dread.)

Of course, I was also going to do this with Travis! With no point of reference or idea about how this would turn out I was taking a risk. In the past, I've wanted more of a guarantee of success. How much have I missed by wanting that? A lot. There's no way to ever know the outcome. Life just doesn't have that option.

Once I said yes, I put on my overthinking hat and started to prepare, predict, and ponder! Brainstorming, planning, and talking to everyone about where they'd traveled before was my main conversation in the world. My lack of education about where we were going or what I needed to take with me, or where we'd be camping, led to lots of research - and I love research! All of this lovely adrenaline and excitement left me buzzing with joy and possibility. I was inspired and then...?

Travis called. And with exuberance, I joyfully shared my new wealth of knowledge. I quickly learned that my ideas were not his ideas. I had a small picture of what we were going to do. He had huge, inspired, let's not miss-a-thing ideas about what type of adventure we were going on. He was annoyed by my suggestions. I was annoyed by his lack of interest in my research. He said a firm NO to my limited view of our itinerary.

You see, I thought we'd be traveling to one or two national parks and then head back to Telluride, where he was living. That would be more than enough for me. The answer? Nope. And then he mentioned that we'd be starting in Eugene, Oregon, and then drive up the coast to Washington State and the Hoh Rain Forest. I was taken aback. The distance was staggering to my inexperienced "road trip!" mind. My resistance shot up. I was defensive and uncomfortable. And that's when he hung up.

What was I getting myself into? That first yes felt great but now I was facing a wall of resistance. Did I want to say yes to something I wasn't sure I would like? And what was Travis thinking?!!! Looking back, I realize I was trying to keep things small. Mentally manageable. I was walking into unknown territory, and underneath I was terrified.

Did I mention that even though I think I'm brave, I'm actually a seasoned scaredy-cat? I was about to face my ingrained upbringing, my patterns of comfort, my go-to responses that have always kept me safe. I felt like I was taking my parents, grandparents, aunts, and uncles along with me, their wise words etched in my soul. I was also weighing my options. Could I back out and say I hadn't already bought my airline ticket? Could I still change my mind?

No. Not now that my new *Bravery Becomes You* mindset had been activated. I wanted this. I had no idea that the power of change could feel so good. I had just experienced the first hint of what bravery could do to my confidence. My decision was firm. I was going on this trip no matter what and I would disappoint myself if I turned back. Considering the other option of a normal, typical "same old" summer made my answer clear. I wanted to live in a new way like never before.

After he hung up, a few silent, irritated, anxious days passed, and we let go of our differences. We were back on track. I wanted this story to work out.

I was also facing adamant confidence from my son. Our roles were reversed. He knew better. He knew more. He could look out for me for a change. (I liked that.) And later, when I discovered his reasoning for being so clear about his larger-than-life itinerary, I understood his stance. But for now, I followed my brave intention. I said a shaky yes.

GETTING BRAVER—WHAT I LEARNED ABOUT FEAR: *Any size YES works.*

My beautiful brave yes. It might have been shaky, but the energy was strong. It felt good.

But before I said yes, my typical wavering needed a commitment to action. Words weren't enough. I was afraid.

I knew I was stepping out of my comfort zone, and I had found good reasons not to go, like: "This was not what I was thinking when I said yes!" or "Who travels without an itinerary" or "Maybe this is a sign to stay home." I was confronting more fear than I had bargained for.

And backing out? You could say I'm a "backing out professional!" For big things and small. Exercise? Tomorrow. Write my book? Tomorrow. Read one of the many books I just picked up from the library? Tomorrow.

Like always, when the first signs of doubt showed up, I was stuck responding with my old patterns of thinking that shouted, "WARNING. TURN AROUND. THIS ISN'T SAFE. CAMPING? ARE YOU KIDDING?"

Even a little bit of fear's powerful suggestions like "That's not what you really want," or "Maybe you made that decision too quickly," are usually enough to make me question my feelings.

We all do it. We talk ourselves out of what we want to do. But we don't have to. In all good stories, the hero tries to back out. But backing IN confirms the commitment. Knowing what you value most in life strengthens decisions and makes your YES stronger.

You can't control the outcome. But you can easily commit to action when your vision is aligned with what you value most.

That's what I was hoping!

Your Turn

I'VE ADDED *Shift Gears* to *View from the Scenic Overlook.* Now you'll envision your future and then "shift" to a new level of understanding yourself and where you're going. New considerations and information add momentum to your next steps forward.

STOP #2

VIEW *from the* SCENIC OVERLOOK

AS YOU LOOK OUT over the view of your future (activate your imagination), there's an invisible but powerful backdrop running behind what you see. Your values! When they are in focus and match your actions they make whatever you're doing satisfying and meaningful. So what do you value most? Here's a list to get you started. Feel free to add your own. Are the values you chose a good match with your vision of the future?

Adventure	Enthusiasm	Creativity	Faith
Connection	Authenticity	Bravery	Family
Loyalty	Dependability	Flexibility	Optimism
Harmony	Beauty	Friendship	Self Respect
Health	Balance	Freedom	Stability
Personal Growth	Compassion	Order	Comfort
Achievement	Courage	Kindness	Giving

SHIFT GEARS: Choose three values that resonate the most for you. Why those?

NEXT:
Going the wrong way?

3

Flying the Wrong Way?

Another Sign?

I WAS READY TO GO! Doubt was still hanging around the edges of my thinking, but excitement and energy were building and I wasn't going to let that go. I was committed.

The day arrived! I was packed, but I admit, I was feeling scattered and overwhelmed with new emotions. It's one thing to think about something, but doing it? That's the problem! And the insecure feeling that I'm not prepared? I know from experience that when I do something new, there's still the "what I didn't think to ask" worry. I knew there had to be something! At the beginning of anything, the learning curve is always greater than I realize, and my loop of overthinking is usually busy handling all those questions.

Enough waiting! Ready, set, go. YES. Now I was ready to test my "new" brave self, and nothing was going to get in the way. Of course, I was wrong. A series of trials were waiting.

My friend Sherry arrived on time to drive me to the airport. I was almost ready. Just throw the last things in a bag and go. I was rushing.

Which meant? Ten minutes from home I realized I had forgotten my purse. I have never *ever* forgotten my purse! Ever. Was this a test? Was fear distracting my intentions?

Chalk it up to a false start. Happens all the time. You get ready to do something, and then like clockwork things pop up and get in the way. Finally, we were off. Here we go again!

Arrival went as planned. My bags were checked. I headed over to security. Get out my license and ticket and? No! Wait. Wait. Wait. No license. I looked through my purse. My backpack. My purse. Again and again. Then, I sat on the floor of the airport and emptied my purse. Nothing. You can't get on a plane without ID. A sign? Another false start?

I traced my steps back to the ticket counter. I was greeted by a less than helpful person who said my license had not been turned in. How was this happening? I never lose my license either! I kept searching in the midst of other travelers jostling to get their bags checked. I kept repeating an astonished "REALLY???" to myself.

Just as I was feeling beyond discouraged, another person said, "Wait. Here it is underneath the check-in counter." It must have slipped out of my hands as I was filling out my baggage name tag. Thank you. Thank you. Thank you!!!

Security again. Fast. Easy. Done. Time to relax. I looked at the flight board. Portland. Gate 15. I had time to grab a coffee. I was early. Once again, I was ready. Life was back to normal.

The airline attendant called the flight. I got in line. They took my ticket. I was halfway down the ramp, and..."Stop!" shouted the flight attendant. "Are you going to Portland, Maine?" I rushed back and said a heart-pounding "WHAT??? NO! I am not." I was about to board the wrong plane going in the opposite direction.

The flight to Portland, Oregon was departing at exactly the same time on the absolute opposite side of the airport. I RAN. My laptop, backpack, and purse banging against my side, I awkwardly made my way around the loop of the terminal. Who cares what I looked like? I had a plane to catch!

At this point, I was hot, worried, and wondering what was wrong with me. I had never gone to the wrong gate either. (Turns out that because I'd arrived at the airport early, the Oregon flight gate hadn't been posted. I just saw "Portland," it had the correct departure time, and so I went directly to that gate. Incorrect assumption!)

Luckily, my Oregon flight was still boarding. But now, the seat I wanted was gone. Only middle seats were left and this was a long flight. Oh well. I was grateful to be where I was meant to be. Happy to sit down, buckle my seat belt, and hope my heart would stop beating so fast.

Anything else? It turned out that the people I sat with were going to one of the destinations that Travis had mentioned. The Hoh Rain Forest in Washington State. This was one of my "too far" places where we might also camp. Discomfort and doubt were ringing in my ears. But luck again…that's exactly where this family was going to camp. They weren't worried about a thing. They couldn't wait. Really? My fear was hanging on their every word.

I also didn't bring a guidebook for this particular area, and they offered theirs so I could get a better idea of what I was in for. Now I'd have some information!!!

I couldn't have sat next to a better set of seatmates. Serendipity was happening. The false start challenge was over. I felt a bit more comfortable about one of our many sites for sleeping. I was on a plane going in the right direction.

I was on my way! Not the easiest morning, but the mishaps became stories. Serendipity added faith to "things happen for a good reason." Good or bad, everything is part of the adventure.

GETTING BRAVER—WHAT I LEARNED ABOUT FEAR: *When things go wrong, you don't have to stop.*

That morning was an obstacle course of mishaps. I've never forgotten my purse, lost my license, or had my ticket scanned successfully as I walked down to the wrong plane. Was I subconsciously sabotaging my journey? Was there a reason I shouldn't go? Was something in the universe tapping me on the shoulder to say, "This was not a good decision and we're sending you big clues." TURN AROUND.

NO. Sometimes things just go wrong. That's it!

That morning I learned two things: Obstacles are everywhere, and I'm often the one creating them from my own limiting beliefs. I'm making myself scared. I'm the one holding myself back.

Here's how I see it. Every time I have something I *really* want to do, all I have to do is wait. And like clockwork, obstacles (what I fondly call "my army of NOs") arrive right on time. Every one of those NOs is a roadblock that tries to stop me.

Those NOs are tricky. They hide behind personal beliefs like, "I'm not good enough, smart enough, young enough, perfect enough." They try to sway me with practical worries like, "not enough" money, time, education, skills. There are many NOs that stop you when you don't want to stop at all.

And the worst thing of all? Most of those NOs aren't even true! They're often based on your comparison of yourself to the rules of your family, society, school, friends, and reactions of others to things you did in the past. NOs love that. They can't wait to tell you that you're going the wrong way or doing the wrong thing.

Of course, sometimes the NOs have good intentions. Their warnings are meant to protect us and keep us safe in the comfort zone where nothing happens. The key is to understand the NOs (sometimes they're right) while keeping your BRAVE VOICE loud, clear, and confident about saying YES!!!

That morning in the airport, I realized that the key is how you respond. All those doubting NOs didn't shake my commitment. That time!

In the past, I've let obstacles stop me. Plenty. The words, "going the wrong way" and "do something else" have always been good excuses and sensible reasons to turn around and stop what I actually wanted to do.

And now? I'm ready. I know that obstacles can throw the commitment to the "call of your dreams" off track. I'm prepared for that army of NOs, just waiting to charge in and stop that first step.

Saying a firm YES when you're surrounded by NOs feels great. And why would anyone say NO when they want to say YES? Kudos for that brave YES!

Your Turn

ADDING TO *View from the Scenic Overlook* (keep that vision alive!) and *Shift Gears* (information that inspires action), you'll now feel the pull of the *Emergency Brake*. (It's what we use when the world says NO to what we want and we listen). Here's a chance to see what's stopping you from taking those essential steps forward.

Remember to write down your thoughts! I'll remind you from time to time.

STOP #3

VIEW *from the* SCENIC OVERLOOK

AS YOU look out at your precious future, see how a big YES energizes action. (I love that joyful feeling). Now close your eyes, see that future, and listen to all those NOs coming your way. Why don't they think you should follow your dream? What obstacles are they putting in your way? Close your eyes. What do the NOs say?

SHIFT GEARS: Pick one NO. Why would it stop you? Can you be prepared the next time it arrives? What could you do?

EMERGENCY BRAKE: The NOs are right. I'm listening to them. I'm not ready to follow my dreams.

NEXT:
Set up the tent?
Well…almost ready.

4

Clarity in Limbo

Postponing Worry

STILL NOT READY. HOPING THAT camping outside in the middle of no-where was just a dream.

You can tell I was still resisting. The anticipation was gnawing at my nerves. Excited. Scared. Excited. Scared. But come on now, I'd had a few weeks to prepare. What was the big deal?

Simple. Fear of the unknown. It doesn't matter what you do or what step you take, the unknown never gives up its secrets until you're right in the middle of it. It's like riding a roller coaster. You might be worried about whether you'll like that big drop that's coming, but you have no idea how you'll handle it until you're screaming with the thrill of it all (or hating it). You just can't know, until you know.

Which is why, after my flight arrived in Portland, I was more than hap-py to postpone my "I don't know if I'll like camping," worries. Our first few days would be a visit to Eugene, Oregon, where we'd stay with my cousins, who I couldn't wait to see. (And yes, sleep in a real bed. No sleep-ing bag...yet.) This would be good. Time to acclimate. I was almost ready.

And that was great because as I stood at the airport, suitcase in hand, I could put fear on pause and keep a lookout for my ride. I only had to wait a few minutes. And there he was. My guide. My traveling companion. My 24-year-old son Travis, who pulled up in his old, well-worn but great-for-mountain roads Subaru, filled to the top with blankets, pillows, camping stuff, clothes, maps, and who knows what. I wasn't sure there was room for my suitcase (my closet for the next six weeks), but he managed to push enough aside and fit me in too!

I was here! His mother. (Was he sure about this?) Ready to go.

But wait. Not so fast.

A preview of my trip was beginning the moment I closed the car door. "There's an interesting place with lots of food trucks," offered Travis as he wove through the streets of Portland. "I think it's somewhere around here." My antenna went up. My words: "I'd rather get going. We've got a few hours to drive to Eugene and I've been up since 5 a.m." He didn't agree. "We don't want to miss this, and I'm sure it's right here. We can get something to eat." Before I could respond with my "This is not how I do things," voice, we were there.

I was still thinking that this isn't how I do things. I like to get in the car and never stop until I arrive. With Travis, there's always something to stop and see. Something you'd never want to miss. I was about to learn how much I've missed in life by choosing to stick to my ingrained patterns of "how I do things!"

And then I saw the food trucks set up in what seemed like a permanent arrangement. I was curious. I'd never seen anything like this before, and the energy of seeing something new, being in Portland, surrounded by people who lived there was a treat. And yes, I wouldn't have wanted to miss this.

I wasn't aware of it yet, but Travis has a "second sense" about what's essential to see. I had never been with someone this good at "getting as much as possible" from every moment of the day. But as I said, I was walking into the unknown, and I was getting to know my "resistance voice" very well. Again, my view of what I wanted to do was "limited." Just wait and see!

I would eventually realize that he was looking out for my best interests. He not only wanted to have the experiences, he wanted me to have them too. He lived at a high-intensity level, and he was taking me along for the ride. It was nice to have someone making sure I was okay for a change. This was a test that included letting go of my control of the situation. I was trying, hoping for at least a B+.

And then we were off to Eugene. I loved the ride—as I would for six weeks. My window view was always new, and I was transfixed by it all. It also felt safe and easy to see the world rush by from the comfort of this overstuffed car. It's safe in a car, right? More on that later.

For now, I was content and happy. Being with family meant so much to me. It was the best feeling I could want, and it was comfortable! Getting to see Eugene, going on a hike, and eating great food was perfect.

This was also like (if I want to be dramatic) being at base camp before a big climb. We still had to prepare and get ready. Hiking poles? Never thought about them before, but I bought a pair. And the rest of our gear? We went to every Goodwill and second-hand store in Eugene and yard sales too. We bought chairs, guide books, a rain jacket for me, and one of my favorites, a sleeping bag that had belonged to a professor at the University (yes, I washed it). The last name that was printed on the outside of the bag? LOVE. I took that as a positive sign. We were given a camping pillow and a nice inflatable pad to put under my sleeping bag.

This was my kind of fun. Second-hand is my happy place.

I also bought a journal to record my thoughts. Ready? I think so. Fun. Absolutely.

I still wasn't sure about what was about to happen (especially camping), but my subconscious was thinking about it. Insecurity? Nothing that the best Chinese food I've ever had couldn't cure. Tomorrow we'd begin. We were almost ready! Oh boy.

Almost ready. The feeling of being on the edge of something, but not quite there, is so familiar to me. I say it all the time, "I'm almost ready."

"When I finish working on this book, I'll be able to get out of the pajamas that I've been wearing for days. It will be soon. I'm almost ready."

"When I get organized with all my projects, I'll start going out more with friends. I'm almost ready."

"When I throw out all my clutter and old clothes and more…It will be soon. I'm almost ready."

"We're about to go on our camping trip, but we need a few more things, and then I'll be good to go." I'm almost ready.

In fact, "almost ready" seems sensible. Smart. Right? After all, I have a lot to do and a big to-do list that grows daily. As an entrepreneur and coach, I have clients to talk to, follow-up work to be finished, and oh, I can't forget—there's all that time I need to spend procrastinating. And then there's that word that's a real action stopper. "Perfectionist."

I feel like I've been "almost ready," my whole life.

GETTING BRAVER—WHAT I LEARNED ABOUT FEAR: *Someday never comes.*

My patterns of living were becoming clear. There was a lot on my someday list. Like writing a book when I haven't written a word, or losing weight when I haven't eaten less, or being in great physical shape when I haven't exercised, or wanting to travel, but I haven't figured out where I want to go. Did I think something magical would happen and all those things would just somehow come true? Yes, I believed that.

So all this getting ready was fun and fine, but I was suddenly aware (again!) that my high anxiety about camping was revving up. The worry didn't go away. And that's what happens when you never get around to doing what you want to do. The wish to do it never goes away. I think it gets bigger. It doesn't feel good to postpone happiness.

Life around the corner? Waiting to get started? Stuck in the "almost ready" zone? I've been doing that for years. I'd postponed so many things I wanted to do because I wasn't quite ready. And now? Those things I wanted before aren't always what I want now. I always thought I'd just pick up where I left off. It's clear. We can outgrow dreams.

The future isn't offering a free ride. There are new and different challenges and responsibilities. But in the midst of everything, I believe that the biggest, non-negotiable, top-of-your list commitment is YOU. One of your life's biggest responsibilities is remembering that you matter, and so do your dreams. Taking care of you and your future is key. It's time to make yourself a #1 priority.

So what do YOU want? How do YOU want to feel? The old list or a new one?

Bravery to the rescue.

Your Turn

IT'S TIME to add my favorite bravery tool. The *Get Brave Compass,* the ultimate navigation tool that makes decisions clear by asking one simple question, "How do I feel if I do? How do I feel if I don't?" It works like this:

You need to make a decision and instead of listening to your usual automatic NO, you STOP and bring your attention directly to the question you want your compass to answer. Next, feel and see yourself saying YES to the question. Then feel what happens when you say NO. Inspired? Disappointed? Your inner GPS won't steer you wrong.

Here's an example: Consider for a moment that you're mentally wrestling with getting out of bed in the morning to go for the walk you've committed to taking every day. You know you can talk yourself out of going. You do it all the time.

But today is different. You remember your *Get Brave Compass*. You pause and imagine the feeling of honoring your commitment. Or not! You close your eyes and consider how each choice would make you feel later. Now ask, "How do I feel if I do?" (go for a walk) or " How do I feel if I don't?" (stay home). What do your feelings forecast? Your choice. And then a quick YES? NO? YES? NO? seals the deal.

I used this technique constantly on the trip to make decisions. (I can be very indecisive). Now, it's a compass I use every day. (Want to learn more? Check out *Three Brave Tools* at the back of the book.)

STOP #4

VIEW *from the* SCENIC OVERLOOK

AS YOU look out at your exciting future, it's time to ask—what makes your heart sing? What do you love to do? What's on all those lists that you still want? What do you want to add? Include everything from dancing to working, shopping, being with friends, talking, walking, eating well, traveling, and reading. Close your eyes. What shows up? What feels good? Or not.

SHIFT GEARS: Note something you'd like to try. What step could you take?

EMERGENCY BRAKE: I don't need to add anything. I'm fine.

COMPASS CHECK-IN: I'm ready to wake up my dreams! or Maybe next year.

Now consider: How do I feel if I do? How do I feel if I don't?

Yes? No? Is it still a GO?

NEXT:
I was ready to GO!
Camping here I come!

PART II

Discovering Freedom From Fear

5

Fear, Fireworks and a First!

Driving Over the First Threshold of Scared

WE'RE OFF! IT WAS REALLY going to happen. I was about to go camping in a small three-person tent with my 24-year-old son. I had no idea where that would be or what it would be like. All I knew was we were going north. Wrong. NO, we were taking a four-hour detour south. There was a special place to swim on the Smith River, where Travis had been before and he wanted to show me. AND SO… let's add on a quick side trip to see some of California's famed Redwoods. South? A longer trip? It made no sense to me at all!

My thinking rut was about to crack wide open. This was just a tiny first step of becoming aware that I have strong opinions about things I know nothing about. What I don't know scares me.

Was it a bad idea to drive south when we were going north? Not when I saw the river and the Redwoods. The awe journey had begun!

River time! I grabbed my bathing suit, changed in the car (something I don't like), and got to the water's edge. It was COLD. Go in?

Compass check-in for me: How do I feel if I do? How do I feel if I don't?

My auto pilot said, "NO." My feelings said, "YES. You're here, don't miss this. Don't go sit on the rocky beach with all the other families, while Travis swims." So with a tentative yes as my guide, I carefully and slowly got myself halfway in and was just about to turn around and get out, when I heard myself say, "Halfway isn't IN!"

Which is why in the middle of a school of kayaks paddling by (and not many swimmers because it was so cold), I did it. I dove in. And right at that moment, I knew how I wanted this trip to be. This was my story and I planned to participate. My compass would be my reliable guide!

I had committed to being brave even when I was scared of being uncomfortable. No more sitting on the rocky beach waving to Travis while he enjoyed the experience. I didn't want to do that anymore. I was so used to saying NO, even for little things like not wanting to be cold. It felt good to say yes as I sat chilled and wet on the pebbled sand.

I watched a very loud family enjoying their day, and while I felt annoyed at their intrusion on my desire to enjoy the scene, and have it my way, I was also interested in their personal dynamics. Everything was part of this moment. What I liked and didn't like were like teammates. Accepting that made the day richer in emotion. There was a story going on here. It wasn't just me looking and commenting in my mind. I was part of an afternoon at the beach...all things included.

What was I worried about? Cold water? A long drive? Trees? I was in new territory, and my tendency to resist was activated.

I wasn't sure where we were going, but I decided to "go with the flow" and not worry (or at least try).

And wasn't it enough that the sky was blue, the sun was out, and we were cruising toward adventure...oh yes...and my first night camping! That's what I wanted, right? No problems with doubt! Life was a postcard as we drove through the Redwoods.

Finally, we were headed to the coast and yes, a turn UP, going north. A right-hand turn and we were back in Oregon, driving up the Oregon Coast toward huge sand dunes and an always-trusted, favorite place for me...the ocean. But when we got there and out of the car, I was facing dunes like mountains.

To see what was on the other side, I had to climb up. Did I want to? Not so much. This was harder than I imagined. It was kind of like walking in deep snow up a slope. Of course, Travis flew to the top and ran down to the ocean. After saying, "How do I feel if I do? How do I feel if I don't?" I chose to climb the dune but then stay perched in the blowing seagrass, loving the ocean view from above. I could have rationalized a nice walk down to the water as good exercise, but it was more than that. My knees weren't happy. 24 is not 64. Reality check.

I'm sure I'll be saying "spectacular" a lot. But yes…it was spectacular.

Anticipating "what's next" was hovering over my experience, but who cares about that when you're headed directly into dinner time! Where to eat? Who knows? A left turn took us to a small restaurant, located in a marina overlooking the sea. A local, no-frills place. We agreed as we stood in the roaring wind…this was our style. We felt lucky to have found a treasure.

A quick delicious meal and we were on our way again. We were getting close to the hour of the setting sun. My first night camping was like an insistent pulse pushing into my thoughts.

Uh oh. Do I like this? Travis had some idea of somewhere he'd heard would be a good place to pitch a tent, but he wasn't sure exactly where it was. He just knew it was a beach. Really? Again, not what I had in mind. But before I could worry excessively, we arrived at a beachfront parking lot where we sat for a moment next to a handful of cars as a dense fog rolled in. "Here?" I asked. "Are you sure we can sleep on this beach?" I heard myself say several times. The unknown was calling out "Not here. This doesn't look right." But Travis seemed totally at ease. "It's fine. We just have to leave by morning," he said. GREAT (sort of). I didn't have much choice. It was time to set up our hotel for the night.

Within minutes we were hauling our stuff through the sand and choosing our spot. We set up the tent in the fog, which made seeing the beach questionable. Handing Travis an assortment of blankets and pillows and sleeping bags was easy. I simply followed his calm directions. There was order in this jumble of stuff and Travis was very organized about what we were doing. He had a plan. We had arrived!

Chairs in the sand, a beer in hand, a review of the day, and yes…it was time to go to sleep. I could barely see anything on the beach except a few fires. Barking dogs and the distant sound of talking sang with the tune of the waves rolling in. And what? Waves rolling in? Yup. I was worried. There was a very high tide line not so far away from us. Who knows how high it would go tonight?

We crawled into the tent. There were small lights on the inside "roof" of the tent which added a twinkling joy to my thoughts of impending disaster. It felt like a holiday celebration that was also accented by booming fireworks going off in the distance. I'm not sure this was a party, but I was enjoying myself. I was pushing concern aside. It all felt good.

The blankets were thick and warm. Inside the tent it was cozy. It was also becoming very clear that happiness was a choice as I not only ignored my worry, but also the sand that had stuck to my feet. It's just sand, right? "Just don't move and you won't feel it," seemed like a good idea. I wasn't about to seem like a fussy mom. I was going to be a resilient camper. "So far, so good" was all I could think as I instantly fell asleep. But I woke up in the middle of the night with that worry again. I was still thinking about that high tide approaching. Would we be washed away? Okay I know that wasn't probable, but possible. The imagination is a powerful storyteller.

As I lay there thinking, I remembered the warnings that I'd received when I was trying to decide to go on this trip. Right now in this sleepless moment, two stood out. "You're too old." And, "Lying on the ground will hurt." Was it true? Well? My legs ached. Ached so much that I couldn't ignore the pain. The hard sand was not the best bed for me. I didn't want this ache to be true, but after trying many ways to get comfortable (despite the scratchy sand), I decided this was what I was in for, for six weeks. I was going to handle it, no matter what. My body would just have to deal with it. And NO...I was not too old.

With that, I fell back to sleep. And—Cheers! Morning. I made it. I lived. I was a camper with one night checked off my list. Everything was okay. And my aching legs? There was hope! Travis started to make my side of the tent thicker and thicker with blankets each night. He was barely sleeping on anything a week later. But he's 24, right?

More than anything, I felt relief. It might seem crazy to anyone who's camped, but for me, this was a big deal. This was my brave journey, and unlike other things at home where I wanted to show that I was "strong and knowledgeable," I wasn't afraid to say I was afraid. I was proud of myself. I did it! Oh yeah, small detail. I'd have to do it again!!!

I'd stepped outside of comfortable and accepted discomfort. I'd crossed a threshold that required action. And here I was. I'd grown in some little tiny way. I could feel it.

GETTING BRAVER—WHAT I LEARNED ABOUT FEAR: *I was afraid of being scared.*

Weeks of worry led up to this one point. And what was all that worry for?

My big revelation? I was afraid of fear.

I didn't want to be somewhere and not be able to handle it. I was used to being in control, prepared for any outcome. I didn't want to be embarrassed or show vulnerability. And here I was with no skills or experience. The unknown was scaring me and I didn't like that feeling. I'd run from fear so often that I was afraid what would happen if I allowed it.

One thing was clear. I worry. A LOT. One concern can quickly escalate into a large list of what can go wrong. It's like my negative intelligence has been collecting data for years. Kind of like a computer. All I have to do is search "careful" in my mind and a list appears. Some are things that have happened to me. Some I've learned about as a citizen of the world. The media, friend's experiences, and even conversations with strangers are full of, "You wouldn't believe what happened." If every chapter of life has a cliffhanger ending, do I want my life experience to be anticipating disaster? It's easier to just say NO.

So being afraid of fear is perfect. Covers everything. It's like I have my own 24 hour-a-day security guard protecting me and my happiness.

But...it doesn't make me happy. It makes me scared and more scared. Afraid of being afraid has been my theme song. And I have allowed it.

How often have I missed out because I didn't want to be scared? Lots. And lots.

And so that night in the tent I put my stress on alert. Things were about to change. *Destination Scared* is not where I wanted my future to go.

Saying "YES, I'm doing what I want because I want to," is my commitment to ME. Going toward experience, instead of running away feels much better. YES is my pleasure.

The same choice can be yours.

Seeing fear for what it is allows you to be in control of how you react to what scares you. Sometimes the worry is valid. It can be a sign of danger and it's important to acknowledge that. And if that's true? Say NO!!!! But more often, fear is a habit that keeps you feeling safe when that's not in your best interest. It's not what you want.

I see fear like this. It can be one of three types:

Safety Fear: "Don't touch a hot stove, don't forget to brush your teeth, don't drive too fast, don't forget to pick up your children (or grandchildren) from school, and don't forget to pay your bills."

Fear of Going Out of Bounds (based on society's values and a whole lot of shoulds we've been hearing all our lives): "Be successful (our way), grow up, go to college, have children, get a job, look this way, live only in these areas, and do what's appropriate."

Inner Fear (based on worry about our own limitations): "I'm not good enough, smart enough, skilled enough, pretty enough, talented enough, strong enough, and so much more."

Fear has a one-track mind.

In the first half of life, the "rules" of life called for creating a safety net that made you feel "you're doing well in the world" and "you're doing the right things." There would be a reward for a job well done. But now, that cycle of living has changed. Those fears aren't appropriate. They've lost meaning and purpose. So the question is, "Can you say goodbye?"

Can you look fear in the face and say, "Excuse me, I didn't hear what you were saying. I wasn't paying attention." I think I hear a YES calling, and it's loud.

※

Your Turn

THE FINAL add-on to your journey is the *Brave Travel Tip.* Words to inspire your adventure. That's it. Just enjoy!

STOP #5

VIEW *from the* SCENIC OVERLOOK

Standing side by side with your YES, it's time to see your future alongside the fears you may encounter on your road trip to happiness. What FEARS come into view? Make a list. Write them down. As many as you want. Big, small, any type. Fear of failing, fear of loneliness, fear of vulnerability, fear about speaking your mind, fear about not taking a shower for weeks (oh, that's mine). Close your eyes. What do you see?

SHIFT GEARS: It's time to have a talk with your fears. Tell them to be on alert. You're reevaluating their message and you'll only be listening to valid concerns. What will you say?

EMERGENCY BRAKE: Fear answers back, I don't care.

COMPASS CHECK-IN: I'm saying YES to happiness or NO always stops me.

Now consider: How do I feel if I do? How do I feel if I don't?

Yes? No? Is it a GO?

BRAVE TRAVEL TIP: YES is my driver.

NEXT:
Is this legal?

6

No Place to Sleep

Break the Rules Lullaby?

GREET THE DAY! IT'S TIME for another nonstop - every minute - adventure and I'm about to discover our morning ritual.

Put everything back in the car. What fun hauling everything through the sand. And what about brushing my teeth? Washing my face? Forget about it? Become resourceful? YES. A cup of water poured over my toothbrush was good enough. I could brush my hair in the car. No washing my face this morning. I'd survive. I was about to do this for six weeks.

I also noticed that we were not alone. The other members of our beach sleepover were also heading out. In the light of day, we all looked scraggly, rumpled, and still waking up. And how did we look, this mother and son team? No one seemed to notice or care that I was the only "older" person there. Maybe I *was* being brave! The only elder sage on the beach? A beachcomber with painful knees? (Getting in and out of the tent was a journey in itself). Sleeping on the grey, wet beach was an interesting type of fun. No matter what, I was proud of myself. The first bloom of confidence?

In the car, I studied the map, in what would become our very well-worn, falling apart atlas, and tried to memorize the image of where we were. Sometimes those maps were my only anchor to feeling grounded.

As I settled into our drive, the realization that I didn't have much to offer except "you're driving too fast" and "turn left" here, was new for me.

I like to participate. I'm a "let's look at things a million ways" over-thinker, but for now, that voice was lacking any relevant "know-how." I was not in charge, and I wasn't the expert. Did I like this new way of being? Would it be possible to let go and trust that "all would be fine?" Not easy at first, but I would get an A for trying. And the truth? I was beginning to relish the experience of not having to figure out anything. I'd been handling everyone's future for so long, making all the plans, making sure everything was just right, and now I was getting a break. Could I handle my new role in life, "the mom" along for the ride? Nothing to think about except our next stop and where would we sleep? It was almost startling to consider how much of my adult life had been spent "hovering" and worrying about outcomes. What a wake-up call. Was I a "control freak?" Probably yes. Could I switch roles? Let's see!

Postcard living was turned back on. The drive. The ocean. The rocks. The rough, majestic beauty around every curve was inspiring. We soaked in this misty landscape for breakfast, lunch, and dinner. Every moment a feast. The views filled my mind.

It was a scenic meditation. No thinking. No pressure. There was nothing to do but enjoy the views and feel the soaring joy of letting go. Travis was also completely comfortable being in charge. Where did he find such confidence? This was a nice view too. Watching his leadership skills in action was a pleasure.

So up Route 101, we drove. Past Florence, Newport, Siletz Bay, Lincoln City, Cape Lookout, and Tillamook. We have that brand of cheese in our grocery store. Hey, something familiar!

Evening arrived. We made it as far as Astoria, Oregon. A new state tomorrow. Already? Washington State was just across the bridge. I'd never driven this far this fast and seen so much. But now our priorities were practical. It was time to figure out dinner (always a struggle) and yes... where to sleep.

We stopped at the few campgrounds listed in our tour book and nothing was available. Hmmm. Break the rules (I didn't even know what they were) and sleep in a public area (not public lands). As always, Travis found a way around what seemed like a huge problem to me. Who is this child of mine, who quickly spied a tent-size spot by the river?

But we weren't alone. There was a group of kids with a tent and other party essentials who had also made their home down here in this cozy (and I'm sure forbidden) sweet spot of "no trespassing allowed." Would they stay next to us and party all night?

My newbie camper mind was activated and restless with a million nervous ideas. I soon heard myself ask my favorite question, "Are you sure this is okay?" The answer? "Yes." It was dark. We had no choice. So up went the tent. In went the blankets, pillows, sleeping bags, and jug of water. Once we were zipped in, cozy without the outside view, we listened to the wind buffeting the tent, set and ready for whatever was going to happen. Which was nothing.

In about a half-hour the party group left, and there we were. Alone in the dark. Alone!!! In a nook down by the Astoria Waterway, falling asleep to the lullaby of nature and the tall reeds of grass rustling. Who knew what else was out there. Was this legal? Would anyone else arrive? Would we be arrested? Me? Worry?

Falling asleep solved that question. I survived another night. Good night, Travis.

GETTING BRAVER—WHAT I LEARNED ABOUT FEAR: *Fear stretches thinking.*

How did I like my 2nd night of camping? Not much. We were somewhere we weren't supposed to be. This wasn't out in the woods where camping is accepted. This was in a random spot next to a river and a city. My history of this skill was zero. My safety alarm was on high alert.

And yet?

I did it. I had to let go of my preconceived ideas about what was acceptable.

So I learned a few things. First, fear is not a fact! It's an emotion. There was no reason to be scared just because this was unfamiliar and didn't go along with my rules of safety. I knew there was a different type of problem solving I could use. I could stretch and reach for new ideas and new reasoning. I wasn't stuck at all. It's easy to be stuck at home. I feel that way a lot. Stuck. Give up. Good excuse. Maybe it didn't have to be that way.

Here my experience required bigger thinking. And you know what? It wasn't hard. I had to go beyond my autopilot answers and listen to new options. And so I tried this: maybe it *was* safe down by the river. Maybe this *was* a perfect place to sleep with a nice breeze blowing. Waterfront? Hey, that's my favorite! I stepped out of "what this should be" and looked at "what was".

Fear is such a narrow-minded NO. It doesn't like what it doesn't like. That's it. But to stretch, use creative thinking, and consider a different point of view often makes it clear that worry is based on outdated thinking. If you don't examine your thoughts, you can easily forget to upgrade your opinions. We are all very capable of reassessing the emotions behind facts.

What a relief! Just because I'm uncomfortable doesn't mean I'm not safe. I want my decisions to be based on an expanded assessment of each situation.

I think of it as inner stretching. A new yoga pose for facing fear? "Hello fear...meet downward dog!"*

*a yoga pose

Your Turn

FROM NOW on Your Turn will include the following:
1. *View from the Scenic Overlook*, your vision of the future.
2. *Shift Gears,* a step forward. 3. *Emergency Brake*, a step back.
4. *Compass Check-In,* the accurate way to make decisions that feel good.
5. *The Brave Travel Tip,* offering words of inspiration.

Remember to write your thoughts in your journal.

STOP #6

VIEW *from the* SCENIC OVERLOOK

LOOKING OUT at your future, consider this: "What can fear do? Is it real?" Take a moment and review the fears that showed up at Stop #5. Pick one. Now ask, "What could happen if this is true? What's the likelihood of that happening?" Then ask yourself, "How can I see this in a new way?"

SHIFT GEARS: Fear of the unknown can create problems that will never happen. How would your typical day change if you removed the power of fear?

EMERGENCY BRAKE: The unknown is a danger zone.

COMPASS CHECK-IN: Stretch beyond fear? or Stay stuck?

Now consider: How do I feel if I do? How do I feel if I don't?

Yes? No? Is It A GO?

BRAVE TRAVEL TIP: Time for fear to sit in the back seat.

NEXT:
My hidden story.

7

The Story I Didn't Want to Tell

You Go Girl!

I DEBATED WHETHER OR NOT to tell this part of the journey. It seems kind of personal. But hey, I'm brave. Right? And this part of my trip was important to me. It's one of the reasons I almost didn't go. But I knew you'd understand that in the middle of the night, I often spent a long time thinking....

"To pee or not to pee?! That is the question." After all, it was very dark outside. Who knew what was lurking outside the tent? Or under the tent? Or around the corner of the tent? Or hiding behind a tree? (I know... too much worrying.) I always wondered if I could "wait until morning." But the answer was always NO. And, I had to go outside at least 2 times during the night. This was an ongoing reality for six weeks. And the unknown always offered new considerations, like the time when a man in a grocery store answered my "anything to be concerned about?" question with a simple answer. "Not much," he said, "But look out for scorpions." Why? Why? Why? I thought.

But back to the campsite (all of them!). There I was, shoring up the courage to face the dark of night, Travis six inches away sleeping peacefully (oh, why can't I do that?) and me wide awake. Like every night, I grabbed my peeing device (I'll tell you about that in a minute), unzipped the tent, and found my flip-flops which I slapped on the ground several times to announce my arrival to the animals waiting for me! Then I pulled myself up off the ground, knees rebelling, left the tent as quietly and quickly as I could (so bugs wouldn't slip inside), and found myself standing in the dark. Ready...to pee. And that's that. Maybe TMI (too much information)...so be it.

The story of my courage facing the call of nature began back home. As I've mentioned, my knees hurt. I don't have the options of "how to pee in the woods" that most easily enjoy (i.e. squatting). It was a real "do I want to go camping?" stopper for a journey that was mostly about sleeping in public lands, where the only human resources were the ones we provided. So I did what I usually do...research. It turns out that women who camp are very interested in this subject. There's a lot of talk and info on the web about how women answer this call in the night.

I discovered a whole new world out there of women who camp. It was inspiring. These were women who knew what they were talking about. They shared lots of "how-to" information including the answers to my pressing question. There were options, reviews, pros and cons, and advice about the products I was considering. And with information in hand, I was ready. There I was, the new expert camper standing (or maybe hiding) in an aisle at REI, shyly asking a nice young man (I pretended confidence), "Do you have any female urinary devices?" Without a blink, he showed me where they were! I had to laugh. Amidst tents and sleeping bags, freeze-dried ice cream (which was always on Travis's Christmas list), and assorted camping gear, I had solved one of my greatest worries about this trip. Peeing outside at night in the dark. I was happy. I had just solved a problem. I was brave! I could pee standing up! Yah!

So how did it turn out? A favorite story happened right at the beginning of our trip on the night we set up our tent in rain forest territory. In this jungle of wet dripping trees— not only an unfamiliar setting but a place where witches and goblins might lurk!—I knew I'd have to get up at night....and pee.

Outside was a biting frenzy of hungry bugs who loved me. Any exit or entrance to the tent would have to be fast.

Looking back, it must have been during one of my quick entry and exits, that something happened to a clear plastic part of my "peeing device." In the morning I discovered it was missing. After packing up the car, we spent at least half an hour looking for it. It was clear. Invisible. It was hiding. It was gone. I couldn't believe it. But being brave, I spoke new truth. "Let's forget it. I'll figure something out." To which Travis responded, "We have to find it. You said it was the whole reason you could come on this trip."

Oh, dear. I don't even remember talking to him about it, but he's also very intuitive, and well, I probably had said something. So there we were mother and son, searching together, in desperation for the saving grace of our trip. I would have loved to see a movie of us. Mother and son, bonding on a quest for meaning in life!

We never found it. But in the next town where we stopped for lunch, they sold them in the gift shop. "Hey Travis, look what I found. This one's called a 'Go Girl'"...Perfect words for a camper like me.

You Go Girl!

GETTING BRAVER—WHAT I LEARNED ABOUT FEAR: *Being vulnerable is lonely. Until it's not.*

My "story I didn't want to tell," was about sharing something that seemed private. Was it appropriate? Was I silly to think it was inappropriate? Why do I think I can't share? You won't like me anymore?

Bravery changes all that. I used my "how do I feel" question, and instantly knew I wanted to share this "small" moment, because for me getting up at night, pushing myself up off the ground, unzipping a tent, zipping it back up to keep bugs away, and standing in the pitch dark with who knows what nearby, terrified me, and I wanted you to hear it from me. I wanted you to know that even though my knees hurt, I had cramps in my legs, and yes...sometimes the pee dripped on my feet, it was thrilling to stand under the stars in the middle of nature's vast, wild, open space. Just me. Alone.

I was also putting risk to the test. Yes, a bear could have mauled me, a scorpion bitten my foot or a snake wrapped around my leg. But at that one moment, I held all that aside. Peeing outside was a stellar moment.

Of course, I am vulnerable in so many ways. It's all mixed in with my worry and the many ways that my doubts show up. Any time you take a risk or walk over the threshold of change, you're vulnerable. But when you can stand for a moment in your brave commitment and be there for YOU, all that vulnerability becomes part of the scenery. The reward of being willing to try is great.

And now that I'm back home, I realize that speaking out loud, saying what I want, and believing that I'm willing to take a chance, reveals vulnerability for what it is. It's a hiding zone where so many of us retreat and miss the opportunity to take a chance on who we are. It's easy to do.

Being honest helps vulnerable secrets come out of hiding. Often, revealing those secrets connects me with the world because I discover that lots of people feel the same way. I only thought I was alone.

Like when I saw a "Go Girl" on sale at Office Depot. Yes, really! I had to laugh. I even bought it for a friend that day. If people buying printers and paper can be comfortable in the checkout lane, can't I?

What about you? What's the story you want to live and tell and share? Will all those vulnerable emotions stop you? Will you worry about looking silly? Too old? Not smart enough? Foolish? A poor decision maker? Or everyone's all-time favorite…I'm not good enough? Will you be criticized for doing something risky, like selling your house and traveling for a year, or being content to stay where you are, choosing to sit and read all day? Whatever you want to do, big or small, the voice of vulnerability can either stop you or inspire you. It's always your choice what you listen to. Ready to find your own voice and speak it out loud, to you?

Can you let the emotions of your new brave self push you to stand up and say to the world (and to yourself), "Stop me if you dare."

It's time to take your dreams on the road to the future that you create.

STOP #7

VIEW *from the* SCENIC OVERLOOK

LOOKING OUT at your future, decide it's time to speak up and share your dream.

What would you say? How would that make you vulnerable? Write your answers to these questions so you can see them in black and white.

SHIFT GEARS: What happens if you embrace your vulnerability? Imagine it. Be there like it's real. How does it feel? Say it out loud.

EMERGENCY BRAKE: I'm afraid of what other people think.

COMPASS CHECK-IN: Keep vulnerability in hiding? or Release it?

Now consider: How do I feel if I do? How do I feel if I don't?

Yes? No? Is it a GO?

BRAVE TRAVEL TIP: Vulnerability connects you to the world.

NEXT:
Losing myself

8

I Can't See

A Foggy Notion

GOOD MORNING OREGON AND AN HOUR LATER...goodbye. After we packed up our riverside campsite, we slipped out of town and over the bridge to Washington State. Destination Cape Disappointment and Long Beach. Hazy fog? A new landscape? New fuel for fear? Or Joy? I had never been to Washington State. All I knew was that "this was a great place to eat cherries" but of course, there was so much more.

In minutes we were looking at views that would be etched in my mind forever. We found the beach. Flat. Good for walking. And we quickly made it to one of our favorite places...the water's edge. A beautiful view. NO. Within minutes I could see nothing. Nothing!!! I felt a quick flinch of panic. I was nowhere. Front. Back. Side to Side. In an instant, I was blind in a thick grey fog.

All bearings lost. I couldn't tell where the ocean was. Before the blank wall of gray arrived, I could see the tide that stretched far out. I had walked through shallow water to get to where I stood and nothing in any direction felt different under my feet. No footprints to follow. I didn't know where to go. This was bizarre. And yet just a few minutes later, it became strangely nice as I chose to relax instead of panic and enjoy the "wrapped in a warm grey blanket feeling." A meditation in a perfect nothing of gray.

But that didn't mean I wasn't concerned.

"This is so weird," I called out to Travis. "Can you tell which way is back to the car?" No. "I can't see much," he called out. "But I found our footprints. We can follow them back." I couldn't see Travis either. But as my eyes adjusted I could make out the slight imprint of feet in the sand in the distance. I needed to look closely, but YAH!!! There was a way out. Just follow the feet! We'd survive!!! I found Travis by his voice. We both laughed at how frightening this was. The relief of safety changed my mood as the fog began to lift enough so that we both could enjoy the misty experience of Washington State.

I was glad to have the rain jacket that I'd bought at the Goodwill in Eugene. We were prepared!

Feeling suspended in space and time was something I'd always remember. Except for the few minutes of *scared*, it was a "be here now" moment standing in the middle of nowhere. Just follow my footprints in the sand? A poetic few seconds.

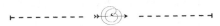

GETTING BRAVER—WHAT I LEARNED ABOUT FEAR: *It can turn off your ability to see what's happening in your life.*

Science says that stress overload turns on the brain's survival mode and turns off the part of the brain that enables higher-level thinking. Mental paralysis is a temporary result. Kind of like stage fright.

That's how it felt on the beach that day. My thinking froze for a moment. It was jarring. Losing my sense of where I was felt like losing my sense of *me*. What do you do when you can't see? When you come to your senses (literally), you see differently. You find other ways to navigate and find direction. Luckily, there's another voice you can listen to (the same voice you've been practicing hearing).

You realize that no matter what's going on or where you are, you always have your inner compass of *knowing* available. Intuition, your gut feelings, your powers of imagination quickly kick into gear when you turn within and simply ask, "What do I do?" I'm always amazed at how instantly answers appear. And they're the best answers I could ask for. They're always right. Reliable. Wow. Who have I been listening to for guidance? Why have I been waiting for answers, when solutions are available whenever I want? Silly me!

That day walking on the beach I also woke up to a problem that often shuts down my ability to move forward. Taking action to activate my future dreams often feels like walking in the dark. You try to figure out if the next step will work. You don't know if it will (you can't), and walking where you can't see the outcome can feel frightening.

What's also true is that I don't always know what I want, but I do know how I'd like to feel. I can use my inner guidance to navigate when the fog stops me. Learning to trust that "inside voice" adds to feeling content and satisfied. I don't have to do anything complicated or difficult. I just have to listen and feel my way. And if I don't like how it feels, I can simply try something else.

That morning, I was momentarily scared without my senses to guide me. It was a fortunate few minutes that made me turn to my intuition as a default GPS and discover the superior guidance I'd always been looking for. I could trust me. I can go forward whether I can see the way...or not!

Letting go of needing a specific outcome makes it easier to take that first step. When your "inner knowing" says it's time to do something. Just look for the footprint to follow.

After all, how long do you want to keep standing there in a fog!

Your Turn

STOP #8

VIEW *from the*
SCENIC OVERLOOK

LOOKING OUT at your precious future, see a picture of promise. Maybe you feel the longing to take action, but you aren't sure how to put your best foot forward? No problem. Your inner vision has the answers. Relax. Close your eyes, choose something you'd like to try, and ask, "What steps can I take?" They can be any size.

SHIFT GEARS: You've got steps to follow! When will you take each step? Energize them with commitment dates. Write this down!

EMERGENCY BRAKE: There's nothing I need to see.

COMPASS CHECK-IN: Live in a fog? or Take an "intuition" step.

Now consider: How do I feel if I do? How do I feel if I don't?

Yes? No? Is it a GO?

BRAVE TRAVEL TIP: Take those action steps before they're washed away with the tides of time!

NEXT:
The haunted forest

9

We're Going to Sleep Where?

1,000 Ways to Resist

THE REST OF OUR DRIVE up the coast led us straight to Olympic National Park, home to the Hoh Rain Forest, a fairyland of ferns and twisted trees that were magical. Something not to miss. I'd made it to the place that I thought seemed too far away when Travis first mentioned it. Another "aha!" moment. My assumptions were incorrect. The drive went by quickly. So why all the worry? Seeing a bigger picture was a better way. Fear had stolen so many moments in my life.

But here we were, spending an amazing few hours walking through paths and forest, and then we were off to Ruby Beach where huge mono-lith rock formations stood tall in tidal pools, wrapped in the familiar mist. Dramatic and craggy. Cozy and rough. A land of contrast. A theme here? Different perceptions create a unique experience. We walked the beach, climbing over many logs piled high, testing my balance. A perfect word in this rugged wonderland. Testing balance. Every moment a tightrope of experience!

Enough thinking. Night was approaching. It was time to find our hotel in the woods. But where? Oh, where? Oh, I forgot. So easy. Find a road. Find a spot. Say yes. Set up the tent. Observe the haunted feeling of night-time in a rainforest setting. Go to sleep. Am I a camper yet? Ask me if I was comfortable sleeping on the side of the road? Not yet. Maybe never.

This was going to take time. And for most of our journey, every night began like this: "We're going to sleep where?" Choosing a campsite was something I never got used to. Driving down dark roads and picking the ideal site to pitch our three-person tent (just big enough for 2) was something that jarred my sense of safety. "This doesn't look good to me," was my general answer as I considered all the terrible things that could happen. Of course, I didn't know what could happen, but I had an instant list of scary stories appear. Travis gave me one of those "you're being a mom" looks and I defended my story. "Look," I said, "You just don't understand. I grew up on the East Coast. You don't just drive down a road and pick a place to sleep. I don't know how to do this!" The unknown can be terrifying. You don't know the rules, the skills, or the safety measures, and I still wasn't 100% sure if my son did.

So, I changed my focus to the road and gripped the seat as the car bounced over rocks while trees brushed and scratched the side of my door (I got used to this too...sort of).

"What are we even looking for?" I asked. Travis dropped a few hints and offered, "Maybe someone has used the spot before, maybe there's a fire pit already there, maybe it just feels right." There wasn't specific guidance like, "This is where everyone sleeps, and it's safe," which would have added to my comfort. Like always, I wanted to participate in those nightly decisions, but I wasn't much help. Except? I was very good at saying, "No...this spot doesn't feel right." Without question, I was afraid of what was out there hiding in the dark. I wondered if a perfect site would show up, even though I didn't know what that was.

If at the moment someone had offered me a comfortable motel room, I might have sighed with relief, but I would have also said no. I knew I wanted to test myself. More than anything, I wanted to be brave. I wanted to believe there was something more to me than what I had always been. Instinctively, I knew that pushing myself was the only way to find out.

"Here?" he asked. "Here is fine," I answered with reluctant confidence.

As the dark rolled in and the rustling bushes sang with the sounds of crackling branches, we worked quickly to get everything set up. Like the nights before, Travis called out the list of tent essentials, and I handed over the makings of what was hopefully comfortable. Blankets, pillows, more blankets, and more blankets made their way into our little home. Our site felt far away from the rest of the world. Yes, we were alone. There were no people anywhere. It was just us and whatever was making the wide range of sounds around us. Travis was a master at assembling the tent fast, and after handing him our ragtag assortment of bedding, we scurried inside and zipped the entrance shut.

I never got tired of the twinkling Christmas-type lights that rimmed the top of the tent or the cozy blankets that were soft and familiar. No high-tech material that was efficient and temperature appropriate. For us it was an assortment of things...and it worked.

Our tent was like a cocoon or a tiny house. Very tiny. And quiet, until that well-known buzzing of mosquitoes began dancing in the lights above. A casual panic in the tent followed as we swept away hundreds of bugs. And what about time? 8:30? 9:00? 9:30? Who knew? My cell phone offered no help. No internet here. So there was only one thing to do. We both laughed at how early it probably was and once again, silence returned. Sort of. The woods at night come alive in a symphony of screeches, hoots, and howls. Just as I closed my eyes, an animal would send out a disconcerting sound that would repeat with a consistent pitch and timing... for hours!

At last, sleep happened....for a while.

Every night brought something new. I didn't always like it. And that's okay.

I was getting braver. I could feel it.

GETTING BRAVER—WHAT I LEARNED ABOUT FEAR: *It doesn't have to stop you.*

It's time to look at how the past is interfering with your future. Longing for change and new solutions for living isn't enough if there's a voice on autopilot directing you to say, "I don't like it. I'm not doing that." Those words are often old messages that you've been hearing and responding to for so long that you not only believe they are true, you don't even think to question them. The problem? They're easy and they make you comfortable. But autopilot behavior is a trap that keeps you stuck.

The solution is to start adding in new positive ideas and repeat them. A lot. The habits and old, outdated reasons you have attached to fear, will eventually soften and release their grip. New thinking will take the place of old.

No question, that old thinking will stop you every time. And why would you want to keep reacting the same way you always have, if those thoughts don't get you where you want to go? They don't even feel good. You don't want to STOP when the reasons are no longer true. You want to GROW!

Change your response, and eventually your brain will make new connections that become what you believe. That belief then becomes who you are in the present, not who you were in the past.

This special time of our lives requires decluttering the past and reevaluating the words you say to yourself behind the scenes of your experiences.

It's time to make introductions: Past Voice meet Future Voice. What do they say? The contrast may surprise you.

Your Turn

STOP #9

VIEW *from the* SCENIC OVERLOOK

AS YOU look out at the scene of your precious future, take a moment to listen to the words that guide you. Who's talking as you look to the future? Your Past Voice? Your Future Voice? To find out, let's ask them.

Imagine your future. What words of fear do you hear? Say them out loud. Are these words just echoes of your past?

Now think of your future again. replacing those words with the ones you *want to hear.* What would cheer you on? Say them out loud.

Write a sentence to yourself using the words that encourage you to believe in the future of your dreams.

SHIFT GEARS: Which words make you feel empowered and energized?

EMERGENCY BRAKE: The past is experienced. It knows best.

COMPASS CHECK-IN: Listen to the voice of the past? or Listen to the voice of the future?

Now consider: How do I feel if I do? How do I feel if I don't?

Yes? No? Is it a GO?

BRAVE TRAVEL TIP: You can change what you think and how you feel. Science says so.

NEXT:
My invisible superpower.

10

This Wasn't on My Shopping List!

Discovering New Eyes

POT SHOPPING? REALLY? That was the next stop on our itinerary. We'd taken the ferry from Bainbridge Island to Seattle and had spent the morning at Seattle's famous open-air fish market, Pike Place. We'd seen it all. It was sample heaven. How many cups of different kinds of apple cider can you drink? Many! Samples of fish eggs (i.e. caviar), that Travis was on the lookout for and found. There was the must-see fish-toss experience. Customer wants a fish. Hurl it through the air. Wrap it up. Sell it. A definite tourist moment. It was getting way too crowded and our camping lifestyle was making city excursions less desirable. Here I was in Seattle in the midst of everything interesting this city offered and I was ready to skip it all and head out to our upcoming destination. Didn't sound like me. Maybe the new me? I liked that idea. I was becoming a camper!!!

But before we left, we found the first Starbucks site in Seattle and also the Pot Stop, Seattle's oldest marijuana dispensary. All legal. So here I stood as my son had a very educated conversation with the nice young women behind the counter. This was science talk. The nuances of marijuana were not my forte...and so I stood and watched. At that moment, I could see, once again, that I like to know where I am and what I'm doing. Or at least I want to look that way. I didn't want to look like "the mother" who was out of touch or didn't know the difference between Sativa and Indica marijuana (see, I'm learning). But there I was—"the mom." Invisible. Awkward. Did I care?

I stood. I watched. And relaxed into a mindset of not judging myself or the situation. I realized how rare that was. Judgment puts huge pressure on everything. Do I fit in? Does this experience fit into what I want? Without that kind of thinking, I was free to see what was right in front of me.

So without judgment, I enjoyed being the observer. It felt like a new superpower. Was I wearing a magic invisibility cloak? I didn't need to fit in. I didn't need to think about what they thought of me and visa-versa. I could enjoy this unique moment and check out the rows of neatly packaged marijuana and be impressed with this professional process. Everything was regulated. Sealed. Strictly business.

So was this a new portrait of my success? I laughed inside and asked myself, "Was this a museum experience?" As long as I wasn't the relic of attention, that idea worked. It was fun to absorb the new mindset toward legal marijuana that was ticking away in acceptance across the country.

In the past, I probably would have sat in the car and suppressed my curiosity. I wouldn't have pushed myself to be interested. But being with Travis opened new views of life I would have typically missed. I might have been interested that this was the first pot shop in the area, but I wouldn't have taken the time to go in.

I liked adding something new and unexpected to my brain. Bravery is often about the little things that change your opinion or viewpoint. Anything that means change, alters the brain (in a good way) if the experience is allowed. Becoming brave was happening right here. Once again, why would I have wanted to miss the first pot store in Seattle? It was a nice souvenir memory.

GETTING BRAVER—WHAT I LEARNED ABOUT FEAR: *You don't have to fit in to belong. You don't have to judge or be judged. And best of all, you don't have to judge yourself!*

So why do we need to fit in? How much of our lives are spent worrying about what people will think if we don't match their expectations? And if we don't fit in, where do we belong? Fitting-in anxiety leads to low self-esteem and confusion about who we are. And the worst? Changing who we are so that everything will be okay. The risk of being left out, not liked, rejected, ignored, or alone can feel important. Sadly, we've all tweaked our originality along the way to please family, friends, employers, or society's story of success.

Standing in the pot shop showed me the way to make *not fitting in,* a perfect fit. I didn't have to figure out how to belong. I belonged to me! And that ME was free to enjoy the observer mindset, where everything holds something of interest or value because you're open and judgment-free. No approval needed. Simply watch, learn, and think whatever you want.

Judging whether or not you or your ideas fit into "acceptable" isn't easy. But switch to the observer, watch the world with a fresh, open-minded view, and you'll not only see new possibilities, you'll feel free to make decisions that are clear and not biased by opinion. That's true liberation!

Deciding the direction of the future based on open-minded/judgment-free options is a big YES for me. Imagine taking a chance on you without the NOs from the past stepping in to say, "Why would you want to do that? or "That's not realistic," or "You're not ready," or "You're too late!" It's not easy to break the habit of interjecting outdated opinions, but when you can...wow...it feels like an "open sesame" moment. Doors open, a new path appears, and there before you is your own brand of personal power and bliss.

What's important is being visible to yourself. We all want to be seen and heard. But now? Being seen by YOU can provide the validation, praise, and satisfaction you've always wanted.

And now you can have it.

Step back for a moment and see. YOU.

Your Turn

VIEW from the
SCENIC OVERLOOK

LOOKING OUT at your future, see yourself as the confident, brave observer. Close your eyes and imagine the freedom of letting go of what other people think about you, as well as your own critical view of yourself. How would that feel?

SHIFT GEARS: The observer can go anywhere. Fit in anywhere. Belong everywhere. How would that change what you do?

EMERGENCY BRAKE: I'll never go somewhere I don't fit in. I'll always care what other people think. I'm very critical of myself and others.

COMPASS CHECK-IN: Open-minded? or Judge every step you take?

Now consider: How do I feel if I do? How do I feel if I don't?

Yes? No? Is it a GO?

BRAVE TRAVEL TIP: You fit in, no matter where you are.

NEXT:
Everything was great. Until
we locked the keys in the car.

11

Can't Go Anywhere Without Keys!

Opening Doors a New Way

YES, TRAVIS LOCKED THE KEYS IN THE CAR! And it was getting dark. We still hadn't found our campsite for the night. So while we waited for the locksmith, we had time to remember and laugh about another "not typical" day.

We thought back to the fun that began after leaving Seattle. We were in search of a view of the San Juan Islands. (We'd determined we didn't have enough time to go there in person, but we decided a glimpse would work.) We stopped for gas, and as usual, Travis ended up talking to a man who knew where we'd find the perfect view. Of course! We followed his directions but took a wrong turn. Just as we were sensing we'd gone the wrong way, sure enough, driving up the road was the man who had told us where to go. He saw us make the wrong choice. Not only did he share his favorite place and directions, he wanted to make sure we found it. Aren't people nice? It means a lot when people are there for you, even in the smallest ways.

We did find the view, hiked down to a spot to see it better, and then..? Hmmm. What's next? Not sure. After a long and beautiful drive, we ended up at a tourist information center. Travis did his typical detailed research questioning. "Mount Baker it is," he said as he got back in the car where

I'd been waiting. "It's not a National Park, but the guy said it should be. It's not to be missed." Bingo. The winning words worked their magic. "Not to be missed" was one of the mantras of this trip.

Of course, to get there, we ended up driving back up the road that we'd just come down. Is there any reason you can't go back to where you just were? Of course, that's what I thought, but who makes all these rules? And when we arrived, there was snow at the top of the mountain. Fabulous views. A great photo spot. I also got to use the hiking poles I bought in Eugene. After all, flip-flops and snow aren't a good match.

Mount Baker lived up to its "better than a national park" status. Another great memory for the day, except we were stuck at a gas station, with a three-hour wait for the key guy. And…the convenience store where we were stranded was about to close! It was getting dark fast. We ended up calling another lock person who came in 15 minutes. Panic averted. A minor glitch, but I still allowed worry to edge into my nice day.

Back in the car, we were off to Mount Baker-Snoqualmie National Forest where, in the dark, we found a spot, once again in the middle of more mosquitos than I had ever seen…or felt! The scenery still had that haunted, beautiful, rainforest look. Those rustling leaves were making my imagination work hard. Is that the wind? Animal? Or maybe a monster emerging from the giant ferns surrounding us? The questions were persistent.

But who has time for that when bugs are forcing a quick tent set-up? We kept getting better at doing this quickly as a team (at least I was trying!). With the tent zipped up, it was time for sweet dreams. Kind of. I was always sleeping with my ear on high alert, ready to handle disaster. My rambling fears were busy making up stories.

Of course, we were lucky. It's the little things that mean success. After all, we didn't have to wait 3 hours in the dark to get into our locked car. We'd found a place. I was grateful to be in the tent. And hopefully safe! What was that noise?!!

GETTING BRAVER—WHAT I LEARNED ABOUT FEAR: *Fear shrinks when bravery grows.*

In such a short time, I could feel myself changing. Each day (filled with so many experiences) I was bursting with positive joy. My fears were getting pushed back. My mind was full of WOW!

I was still scared, but I was moving through it. I wasn't stuck in it. And everything we did added to my bravery bank. There was a reason why.

Did you know that when you accomplish anything, no matter how big or small, your body sends a bit of the chemical dopamine to your brain? And it feels good. It also increases motivation and a sense of satisfaction. And that's what happens when you're brave. Here's why: the more you're brave, the more you *want* to be brave, and the more you *look forward* to being brave. Your body helps by sending in positive chemical reinforcements that feel a whole lot better than what you feel when you say NO. YES, bravery feels good.

Being brave enough to follow your intuition helps sort out the confusing internal paradox we all live with. Your mind says, "NO...you've got to stay safe. Let's not try anything new." Your heart, however, says, "Let's go and grow." Feeling good to the rescue!

For me, that meant enjoying my day and keeping my worries in check at night. I still thought about a bear tearing down the tent, or a mountain lion tracking us, but I could also push that aside and enjoy where we were.

In fact, the happier I became, the more "scared" softened. I appreciated my ability to thrive. I was stronger than I knew. For once, looking to the past was a good reminder that I had powers I could retrieve and enjoy.

Time to take inventory. Have you forgotten how powerful you are?

Your Turn

STOP #11

VIEW *from the* SCENIC OVERLOOK

AS YOU look out at your future, you wonder if you have what it takes to stand up for yourself and your dreams. When self-doubt creeps into your view, stop it by remembering your strengths. What comes to mind? You can add more later.

SHIFT GEARS: Recall a time when you showed strength. Have you experienced loss, betrayal, disappointment, or failure? Have you helped someone else by nurturing their talents? Are you a loyal friend? In what ways were you strong? What did you do?

EMERGENCY BRAKE: I'm not strong.

COMPASS CHECK-IN: Appreciate your unique strengths? or They aren't worth noting.

Now consider: How do I feel if I do? How do I feel if I don't?

Yes? No? Is it a GO?

BRAVE TRAVEL TIP: You're stronger than you think.

NEXT:
Can I take a shower yet?

12

Is a Lake a Shower?

Shampoo Anyone?

WE LIVED! (I felt that every morning.) Another beautiful day arrived and we set off to explore. We began with a drive down a long dirt road. To where? The glory of Mount Baker Lake. And what to do at 7 a.m.? It was time to swim. Of course! And the way in was right in front of us. A boat ramp was calling my name! It didn't take long for Travis to dive in. Okay. Good for him. But like always, I was debating with myself. Forget everything I've been telling you about bravery. Why would I need to be brave and get into this freezing cold water? First of all, I had to put on a bathing suit. Then I had to get in. Did I want to? Here goes...I asked, "How do I feel if I do? How do I feel if I don't?" I DO won.

I love that question. I'm often indecisive and I can spend a lot of time going through an endless loop of pros and cons. But when I ask that question, it takes my busy mind, and puts it right back in a state of focus, looking at the question that's facing me. With laser clarity, I ask and decide. YES or NO. What will it be?

I DO was my decision. But now I had to take action. There were a few people wandering around, so I found an outhouse (not my favorite) and put on my suit. Then off to the water where I approached this lake "Sandy style." Inching in. Inching in. Yes? No? Yes? No? and Yes! I did it! There I was, immersed in a chilly paradise. Glittering sun-sparkles shimmered across the lake, surrounded by mountains, worthy of that national park title. Yes, there I was in this refreshing-beyond-words moment. Did I mention that I'd almost forgotten how water feels? I hadn't had a shower for days. That nice morning ritual hadn't been available. And what about shampoo and soap? Well, let's not go that far. This was a soapless experience, but still? My bath for the week!

It was nice to feel washed and ready to go, but it also felt good to realize I could be "just fine" not washing my face or wearing makeup, or blow drying my hair. It was a treat to simply get up and go. No fuss. AS IS. A new "free to be me" mindset? Yes. It was good.

I also knew that soon we'd stop for breakfast and coffee! I'd have a chance to check out a bathroom mirror, wash my face and rinse out a few things (that would then be spread out in the trunk of the car to dry), and brush my hair. Simple pleasures. I was getting used to a short to-do list. What a gift!

And what a day! We drove through the North Cascade Mountains to the Diablo Dam and then to the brilliant turquoise green Diablo Lake. Magical.

Out of the corner of my eye I saw Travis talking to the nature guides. All I could think was, "Please don't tell him something is interesting, we'll have to go there." A little resistance? Wanting to keep things manageable? Stay on the vague itinerary we'd talked about? A pattern here? A problem? Oh, yeah. My passion for being careful was on alert.

Travis announced, "We're going to Chelan." Where? I was about to find out. Clearly, the guide at the visitor center hadn't read my mind. He said this was another "must-see" site. I said, "Yes. Of course!"

Now you might think that I had no opinions/no say. But I had no idea where we were, or what would be good to see. I had handed over my time to someone with a sixth sense for adventure. It was my choice. And even though letting go wasn't always easy, I kept reminding myself that after years of planning vacations, booking airplanes, and searching for the best places to stay, it was a relief to be off the hook. I wasn't responsible for anyone's happiness or entertainment. This was a treat.

On the way to Chelan, we stopped for lunch in Winthrop, a cowboy-styled town. We ate lunch by a stream, checked out some travel brochures, and wandered around. And that was that.

Next stop—the 50.5 miles of Lake Chelan. Charming. Lots of people swimming/vacationing—a summer resort place. Time for a swim, and then the research began. Turns out that an eight-hour round trip boat ride on the Lady of the Lake to Stehekin is a *National Geographic* recommended "must do" experience. (Gotta go!)

This meant that it was time to start planning the next day's boat ride, which is the only way to go since no roads lead to Stehekin, a valley surrounded by the peaks of the North Cascades. We bought our tickets for the next day and of course had a nice talk with a woman who was closing up. She shared that one of the main activities upon arrival was a trip to the waterfalls. "Everyone takes a bus to the waterfall on Stehekin, but you can rent bikes," she offered. Great. I already knew that following the "group plan" wouldn't be the perfect experience in Travis' opinion, which meant bikes for us when we arrived, instead of the cute red bus that drove directly to the falls.

That would happen tomorrow. Right now it was getting dark, so we asked about where to camp (always last minute) and it was suggested we take the very steep road up to the top of the Chelan Butte. That's what we did. It was not a comfortable drive up. Very steep. Very high. A choice spot for paragliders during the day. (I may have shed a few tears.)

But once we arrived, breathtaking views of Chelan, far below us, unfolded with the twinkling evening lights welcoming visitors into this idyllic summer scene. Perfect spot? NO. No one mentioned the wind. Hurricane force? Not quite, but the wind was so strong that the entire night I felt like we were going to be blown off the edge of our site on this mountain tiptop. The sides of our skimpy home were flapping in the breeze like a kite ready to fly. Beautiful spot. But not a good location that night. There's always tomorrow!

GETTING BRAVER—WHAT I LEARNED ABOUT FEAR: *Fear isn't comfortable. And that's okay.*

So much was great on this trip. I think I'd call it perfect. The reason? All the problems, frightening moments, and discomfort were part of our story. The fact that I could deal with every bit of it, get over myself and my stress, and observe my fear was the best thing I've ever done.

Whether it was the narrow road up to the campsite, or the wind lashing the tent (which also pushed against *me* all night), I somehow managed to deal with it all. The hard parts offered the greatest reward.

I was becoming more flexible! Who knew? I found a bravery trait blowing in the wind.

I'd never really thought of flexibility as brave, but it's an essential skill that helps when crossing every threshold of change. If you don't go with the flow when things aren't what you expect, then the only alternative is to STOP.

"Uncomfortable but flexible" allows new options to appear. "Inflexible" is rigid. It breaks the connection to the growth that's waiting to be experienced.

And although my knees weren't so flexible, my heart was. That was all I needed to climb this emotional mountain that was waiting for my arrival.

So how about you? Have you exercised your flexibility lately?

Are you ready to leave the comfort zone and get into the flow of flexibility?

Your Turn

STOP #12

VIEW *from the* SCENIC OVERLOOK

LOOKING OUT at your future, you know that change is part of what you want. But can you bend your own "inner rules" and allow something new? Rate your flexibility from 1 to 10.

SHIFT GEARS: Flexibility gets you across the threshold of fear. It breaks the habit of your autopilot NO so that YES can allow the flow of opportunity. Think of a time when you bypassed NO and said YES. Did something good happen? Write it down.

EMERGENCY BRAKE: I don't like change.

COMPASS CHECK-IN: Flexible flow? or Stuck in the comfort zone?

Now consider: How do I feel if I do? How do I feel if I don't?

Yes? No? Is it a GO?

BRAVE TRAVEL TIP: Getting comfortable with discomfort feels great.

NEXT:
Serendipity Just In Time

13

Doing it Our Way. Why???

Don't You Trust Me?

A NEW DAY! And we were going somewhere that's not on the typical tourist destination list. Most people I know haven't heard of this isolated paradise or the four hour boat ride we were about to take, headed toward Stehekin, a unique place, home to about 75 permanent residents. The brochure said that cruising the glacial lake surrounded by the majestic cascades was like being in the Norwegian fjords, and I agreed.

When we arrived, everyone got off the boat and headed to the red shuttle bus ride to the famous Rainbow Falls. NOT US!!!

We went in search of the bikes. A few moments later we found the location and in minutes we were on our way. It was fun until it wasn't. I was struggling. But as we turned toward the falls, the lineup of red shuttle bus patrons were just finishing up their waterfall experience which meant that we had the falls all to ourselves. No one to interfere with our one-on-one time with nature. Lucky us! It was lovely. The effort was worth it. Doing it our way was better.

Our bike ride back was easier, and I relaxed into this serene "Switzerland" experience. Alpine beauty everywhere.

A swim, a stop at an organic farm, and the reward of the island's French bakery where homemade delights were waiting couldn't have been better. We were definitely somewhere special…somewhere we couldn't miss!

Time to go back to Chelan. Four hours later we arrived and were immediately back on the road heading to Leavenworth, a fairytale place designed with Bavarian architecture. We ate bratwurst and German potato salad and marveled at this pristine replica in the middle of nowhere. But soon it would be dark. Sorry. We didn't make it to the nutcracker museum! No time. Got to find a campsite.

But where? On the road again with nightfall nearing, we were running out of time. My "where were we going to sleep" worry and vulnerable voices were right on schedule ringing like alarms in my brain. Worry. Worry. Worry. About what? We'll be stranded. We'll end up somewhere we shouldn't be. We'll be eaten by wild animals. I'll step on something alive and scary in the middle of the night. We'll be murdered by a mad man or woman. The list goes on and on, but can I let go? Not right now. The highway was all I could see. I was not sleeping on the side of the road!!!

We stopped for gas. I sat in the car and waited while Travis went into the convenience store to get snacks and pay. What could I do? Wait. Do nothing. Look at the pictures on my phone. Oh well, no internet. And the best option? Let go. Remember that it's worked out so far, why not tonight? Think about how much I worry. And let go. Trust that it's going to work out. We'll sleep somewhere, right? But who will help us? How can we find a good spot in less than an hour when it will be dark? Who will give us advice? Who do we ask for help? 911—"We need a campsite?"

It didn't take long and Travis was back. "Great news," he said. "I just talked to a nice woman who works here. Guess what? She also works for the park service, camps all the time, and knows this area well." He handed me a piece of paper. Directions were scrawled in his barely legible writing with the name of a street where we were to turn left. "She said her favorite campsite is just a few minutes from here. She just camped there." So in the dusky dark, we found a street sign that seemed close to what he'd written down, and we decided "Let's take it." Turn left…turn, turn, turn (can this be right?) keep going, keep going, and just as I was sure this wasn't going to work? Wow—a pristine spot, right by a river. A family was camping nearby too (I do like neighbors). We were set. (FYI...bears like water...did I need to know that right now?)

Tent up. Blankets, pillows, sleeping pad, and my side still getting thicker and thicker (Travis is a good sharer). Good night moon. See you in the morning. Or maybe a few times during the night. Who's out there? I have this down. Sort of. Flip flops ready to warn away whatever might be waiting for me. Flapping them on the ground as I crawled out of the tent. I'm here! I'm nice! Stay where you are!

Dozing off I considered, "Was there any reason to worry?" Probably. "Was there any reason to think this wouldn't turn out fine?" No! Exactly. Could I learn to trust that things would be okay?

Night night. Sweet dreams.

GETTING BRAVER—WHAT I LEARNED ABOUT FEAR: *Fear attracts negative feelings. Trust attracts positive outcomes.*

I couldn't believe our luck. Amazing that we stopped for gas at that particular gas station where that particular woman was working at those hours, and she had just the right information that led us to an idyllic site by a river. Was she waiting for us?

Serendipity was becoming a natural part of our trip: meeting people who gave us the best advice (which we followed), turning down a road that took us to a "not to miss" experience, discovering restaurants in the middle of nowhere that were just what we were looking for. After a while, trusting that everything would work out made every day a surprise party.

The difference between my experience and Travis's is that I hoped that each day would turn out as great as the day before. He *expected* it. He was open. He seemed to gravitate to the best life had to offer. I kept thinking, "How does he make all this happen? How did he know where to go, when he'd never been here before?"

He knew what he wanted. He wanted the experience to be soul-stirring. He wanted to feel that he was experiencing something special. And that's what life offered to him.

He also wasn't wishy-washy. His focus on efficiency and his concept of high-quality experiences was laser sharp. We wasted no time. There were things to see, places to go, people to meet, and we both were in sync with the goal...we didn't want to miss a thing.

Amazing what you can learn from your children! Travis showed me that even though he appeared carefree, he was serious. No stone went unturned as we ventured down roads because they looked interesting or walked the extra mile to find a spectacular view. That extra push. That "too tired to walk that far, but you did anyway," persistence was like the icing on the cake of every moment.

Magic was everywhere. It was always there. You just had to be willing to join in life's treasure hunt and be the seeker. That's how I want every chapter in my life to be. Joy on the road. Enjoying the push to live more. Be more.

Serendipity as the driver works for me.

Of course, there I was worrying or scared that maybe this time we wouldn't find a good place to pitch a tent. But I was beginning to "get it."

This is how I wanted to live.

How about you? Can you give up having "a success plan and an itinerary" before you take a step? Can you trust that tuning into the intelligence of an "open mind," with a focus on how you want the future to FEEL, will add a dash of delight to every day?

Time to loosen the reins on rules? How about a *Bravery Becomes You* date?

❦

Your Turn

STOP #13

VIEW *from the*
SCENIC OVERLOOK

LOOKING OUT at your future, you decide to add some unplanned joy to your day. It's time to make a bravery date with yourself and try something new. What could you do? Go to a movie in the middle of the day? Call a friend you haven't talked to in years? Take a nap. Take a walk somewhere different. Eat ice cream for breakfast? Take a class to learn something new? Name a few things that come to mind.

SHIFT GEARS: Adding "you time" that's out of your normal routine turns off your to-do list and instantly creates an opening for new experiences to come your way. Where can you find time?

EMERGENCY BRAKE: I'm too busy.

COMPASS CHECK-IN: Magic? or Monotony?

Now consider: How do I feel if I do? How do I feel if I don't?

Yes? No? Is it a GO?

BRAVE TRAVEL TIP: Live more. Worry less.

NEXT:
The Other Side of Things

14

When Awe and Disaster Meet

What's Hiding Beneath the Surface?

BACK ON THE NATIONAL PARK trail of experience. First stop, Mount Rainier, the tallest mountain in Washington State and considered to be one of the most dangerous volcanoes in the world. It's on the Decade Volcano list because of its potential impact—deadly for all things living in the area, with effects that could reach from Canada to California. Its last eruptions were in the mid-to-late 1800s.

But who thinks about that when standing before something so spectacular? What did Travis and I talk about at times like this? I'd say it was the language of awe: "WOW," "Amazing," "Can't believe this," "Spectacular," and "Look at all the tourists."

Actually, we talked all the time and what we said was mostly about the moment. What was right in front of us had our complete attention. There was nothing more to think about than beauty and being transformed by experience. Of course, we also talked about maps, meals, and where to sleep, but that (as you've been reading) was often last minute and had our complete focus too. Living in the moment was full and included all emotions from fear to fabulous, but it was also relaxing. Every moment bursting with possibility. My quest to experience bravery was not only revealing a lot about me and how I've been living my life but more and more, I wanted my life to feel this expansive. Travis was the perfect example of thinking big like it was the most normal thing in the world. As I kept noticing, being awake, aware, and present in the moment was how he lived every day.

So how was I going to keep all this wonderful "live in the moment" energy going when I got home? STOP! I could feel the worry coming on, and this mountaintop was no place to activate my loop of doom. One thing was clear. Nothing feels better than being brave.

To be brave you need to overcome, understand, and embrace uncertainty and vulnerability while keeping the high vibe of curiosity, positive emotions, and joy going strong. And the final, essential requirement was action. Nothing happens if you do nothing. This road trip was showing me that at every turn I was learning a new way to live in the world. I could see that everything you do, no matter how big or small, is like an internal action plan that informs and strengthens your emotions, clarifies your feelings, and brings your unique style into focus. Inner growth makes it possible to change your outer world. How you want to live is then created by you and directed by you. What fun. Living from the inside out!

Back behind the wheel…views and views and views took us to Mount St. Helens, which erupted on May 18, 1980. Some say this was the most disastrous eruption in U.S. history. It also created the largest landslide ever recorded.

Our arrival was perfectly timed. End of the day. Tourists were gone. We were able to stand and experience the decimated landscape and the reality of what a volcano can do. Comparing this to Mount Rainier was like seeing the outside versus the inside, where the hidden truth lies. Smoldering power waiting to erupt. A world beneath.

Wildflowers nearby offered the message of growth and renewal—a poetic moment of awe and disaster.

GETTING BRAVER—WHAT I LEARNED ABOUT FEAR: *It can be an awe-inspiring wake-up call.*

Here was the natural cycle of life. Beauty and destruction. Living and dying. Life is always transforming. The message was in the air: every day is strong yet fragile... you never know what's going to happen. Enjoy the moment! What are you waiting for? You don't have forever!

What's hiding beneath the surface of YOU, waiting to erupt into view? Can you hear nature calling? Wake up. Wake up. Things are bubbling, burning, ready to come into view. That unseen life beneath is waiting for your directions.

Standing before Mount Rainier and Mount St. Helens was proof that no matter the outcome, the end result is the natural phenomenon of you. Beautiful!

Your Turn

STOP #14

VIEW *from the* SCENIC OVERLOOK

LOOKING OUT at your future, consider your hidden potential just waiting to show itself to the world. What's been hiding? What's something that's been waiting to erupt and be seen.

SHIFT GEARS: How could you share that potential?

EMERGENCY BRAKE: Nothing is hidden. I know myself.

COMPASS CHECK-IN: Wake up and burst out? or Go back to sleep?

Now consider: How do I feel if I do? How do I feel if I don't?

Yes? No? Is it a GO?

BRAVE TRAVEL TIP: Inner travel is a scenic wonderland. You never know what you'll discover.

Time to write!

NEXT:
**Driving over the edge
of reason**

15

There's Something Wrong with the Brakes

NO is Not On Our GPS.

"I'M NOT DRIVING 11 HOURS to hear a band in a bar!" The idea of traveling 11 hours to hear a band Travis liked was way out of my comfort zone, and I wanted to put the brakes on this one, fast. This was my personal "this has gone too far" intelligence speaking. Travis's idea was a clear NO for me, although I could tell that my NOs were getting weaker. My emergency brake was broken! So I kept a crack open for considering this crazy option.

But I still couldn't stop the brigade of NOs coming my way. Sometimes resisting is a good thing! Right? I was uncomfortable with the proposal. I wasn't even sure if I could sit in a car for 11 hours. It scared me. What if I were bored? What do you do sitting still for that long? Travis saw nothing unusual in the plan. A favorite band, one he'd gotten to know in Colorado, was playing for one night only. To him, there was no choice. This was another once-in-a-lifetime moment. His yes was firm to my no. "Are you kidding me?" I offered. I was silent for a while, trying to think if I could possibly accept this. I was learning that NO didn't have the same ring as it used to, and so I let the concept simmer as I processed the amazing journey we'd just had at Mount St. Helens and Mount Rainier. Now we were heading back to Eugene, Oregon, our kick-off location for this "maybe" long drive. I just kept thinking "We've been in this car for so long. How long is long enough?"

As we sped down the highway, I stared out the window and had plenty of time to think this over. Since Travis always took the scenic highway, every view was a spectacular gift. The majestic world flew by, and I pondered. I didn't know what to say. Except for NO, I had no answer. What was a mother to do? Let the typical loop of doubt and worry shape my decision and ruin the mood of the moment?

As always, the car (filled with its hodgepodge of our home on the road), was also filled with music, our singing, a steady breeze through the open windows, and the joy of "what comes next" waiting on the map that sat at my feet.

The happiness of freedom began to seep into my mind. I started to shift into inner consideration. Slowly that thread of pushing myself to do something outrageous, something I had never done before, and something that seemed completely wrong to my sense of time, generated those butterflies of stress and excitement. They were taking their grip on me as I consulted my inner guru. After all, is there a rule about driving time? Where did my "that's too long" idea come from, anyway?

"Sure, let's do it," I announced.

Now I could sit back and enjoy the rest of our return drive to Eugene, where we arrived at midnight. Luckily, we were staying with my cousin, Chris, in his "something right out of a magazine" perfect guest apartment which was aptly named, "The Stamp." It would have been nice to enjoy for more than the six hours that we had to sleep, but we were actually on a schedule.

Alarm at 6. Car by 6:15. We're off! It didn't take long until I was confronted with my typical conversation. Was this a roller coaster ride? My heart was in my throat as we made our way through the Trinity Alps, along a two-lane highway, a dizzying sequence of hairpin turn after hairpin turn. We were also sharing the road with large trucks and impatient drivers. We needed to be safe, but the clock was ticking too. We had a concert to get to! I did trust Travis, but how about everyone else? Sit back and relax? As always, that's a personal choice, and that's what I tried my best to do. Once I got used to believing that we'd be okay, it became easier to simply appreciate the moment. Nature soothed stress, and we had a stately wall of beauty to calm me on this very long thrill ride!

With the Grateful Dead playing in the background, trucks slowly chugging up hills in my view, and the scenic drive of a lifetime all around me, I let the day unfold. We arrived in Willits, California, in a timely 11 hours. There was history to learn. Willets had gone from bustling to a bit forgotten. Our run-down 70s motel, stocked with tiny bars of soap, worn plaid comforters, and questionable décor, was a nod to the past. And then there was the band we'd come to see. They were effusive in their happiness on seeing Travis. And yes, the music was great. There was plenty of dancing, talking, and meeting new people. I wouldn't have wanted to miss this. Once again, I couldn't help wondering how much I've missed in life by resisting what didn't make sense to me. But for now, it didn't matter. I was pleased that I'd arrived and listened to my new brave voice.

GETTING BRAVER—WHAT I LEARNED ABOUT FEAR: *Resistance is a big excuse not to try.*

Eleven hours turned out to be absolutely fine. And now, after traveling six weeks on the road, I've completely changed how I feel about time and travel. Since this trip, I've taken many long car rides, and never once have I considered not going or not liking the ride. An 11-hour car ride? Let's go! It's amazing how wrong I was about myself and what I would like. My decision-making skills got an upgrade. How many times have I judged without knowing if I was right? Too many.

Now I see the way a limited mindset affects how I move toward the future. How easy is it to say that I can't do something because it will take too long, or it requires too much experience, or I'm already overwhelmed and can't do more? How do I know what I can do, before I even try?

All those dreams of the future can drift into nothing when at first they seem great and then they seem impossible. Can you really sell your house, buy a camper, and travel the world? Can you start a new business with no experience? How about manage to be newly widowed or divorced and be as social as you once were or enjoy not being social at all: recover and move on from emotional setbacks or take care of elderly parents and still have a life? Can you do what you say you want to do instead of talking about it?

Who knows? No one. Lesson learned. Try first. Decide later.

Your Turn

STOP #15

VIEW *from the*
SCENIC OVERLOOK

LOOKING OUT at your future, imagine your vision again. Is it too far away? Will it take too much work? Will it be a bumpy journey? What's the distance you're willing to go? Is that stopping you? Write your thoughts down.

SHIFT GEARS: Name something you want to "try first" and "decide later."

EMERGENCY BRAKE: It will never happen. It's too big an idea. Think I'll skip it.

COMPASS CHECK-IN: Take the risk? or Resist?

Now consider: How do I feel if I do? How do I feel if I don't?

Yes? No? Is it a GO?

BRAVE TRAVEL TIP: Happiness has no due date. Enjoy the ride!

NEXT:
Miles and miles and miles to go.

16

How Fast Can We Go?

How Much Can We See?

SAN FRANCISCO, HERE WE COME! If it seems like we were going fast, we were! I call it millennial speed. But the energy of our trip was so great that it propelled us forward with ease. Similar to the energy it often takes to act, rather than "wait until tomorrow," it felt like I was "in training" for moving toward my dreams, rather than listening to my habits talking me out of taking a step forward. Of course, now I was taking a lot of steps forward, and it made every day a rich experience. I didn't feel like I was missing anything. I was seeing just what I needed to see and we saw a lot. Each day felt like we had an eternity of hours to do what we wanted to do.

Now that I'd recovered from my crisis of driving 11 hours to hear a band in a bar, I was feeling comfortable with the length of our current drive.

Next stop? The Golden Gate Bridge. We drove through the "required" viewing location, took the important photos, drove across the bridge, and found ourselves in Chinatown, trying to decide where to eat. We read reviews, walked around absorbing the colorful, lively scene, and chose the highly recommended best place for lunch "if you're okay with questionable health regulations." No English spoken. Mostly Chinese diners. Talking. Reading newspapers. A community. All while I was trying to choose from a menu I couldn't read. Just how I like it. An experience.

Next, the Eastern Market Bakery, the oldest in Chinatown. Try a little of everything. Why not? Moon cakes, coconut buns, lotus buns... hot, fresh, and interesting. Many were full of red bean paste. I had no idea what we were trying. We took a "to go" bag of goodies. They didn't last long as we binged and laughed till it hurt, as we asked "how much red bean paste can you eat?" Yes, we liked red bean paste!

Onward to Big Sur. Recent mudslides led us on a detour which gave us limited, but beautiful views until we hit a dead-end roadblock. At this point, we were getting used to detours and highway road repairs. It seemed like everywhere we went, we'd see that dreaded orange "road crew ahead" sign which meant we were about to wait a long time for our turn to use the road. (One stop was 45 minutes in the hot desert!) I've never seen so much road construction or had to wait so long. Pausing to be patient when you don't want to be isn't pleasant. Unexpected stops interrupt forward momentum. Delays just add to the amount of time it will get to where you're going.

That part I was getting used to. Long waits, time after time, in every single state, were something we just had to accept. Lots of times, we ended up talking to the people with the stop/go signs. Sometimes they shared useful information after listening to our probably annoying questions: "Where is your favorite beach, favorite place to eat?" or "Where should we *not* go?" Whatever the answers, it always seemed like a good connection. My compassion grew for their day-to-day "turn the sign" jobs, with passing drivers glaring at them for making them wait. I'm sure I've done that too, even when I know the delay isn't their fault.

Then to Santa Barbara, a nicely manicured town and one of the few places where we had to stay in a campground because they had no public lands. We found our site as I watched the plumes of smoke rising into the air from fires not that far away. Oh no. Something to fear again. Fires are a deadly danger in California and getting stuck in a mountain blaze caught my imagination. But instead of trusting that idea, I asked if anyone else was concerned. No one was. Just me. I had to go with that. And hey, they had bathrooms, showers, and people nearby. We set up the tent and filled it up with our stuff. But this site didn't have the charm (did I really say that?) of the rugged, off the road, public lands that seemed populated with nobody but us and the wild things that roamed in the night. I knew, right then, I was changing…getting braver.

GETTING BRAVER—WHAT I LEARNED ABOUT FEAR: *There are lots of roadblocks and detours on the road to happiness.*

So what do you do when you're faced with a big stop sign? Simple. You stop. Usually, you have no choice. It's frustrating. Annoying. And your energy deflates.

As I mentioned, one of our roadblocks was in desert-like heat where we sat in a long lineup of cars for 45 minutes. We were roasting. Using the air conditioning would have overheated the car. We complained. We ranted about this inefficient use of our time and the unpleasant experience we were forced to endure. We were a community of complainers stuck with no way out.

And yet...was the way out, the way in? Digging deep, we managed to accept what neither of us is fond of. Patience. We relaxed into the moment. We talked about our plans. We looked at maps and drank more water! We accepted that sometimes the "outside" world has control. Beyond our temporary situation, the reality of life includes many roadblocks and for endless reasons. You have to take care of a family crisis. Deadlines have to be met. Someone's sick. School's canceled and you've promised to be the pickup driver. A bill has arrived and now you have to reevaluate your budget.

What did I realize? A stop sign outside isn't a stop sign inside. Whatever's going on in your life doesn't have to put the brakes on how you want to FEEL about your future. You can grab all that joy and enjoy it right now. You can conjure up your brave powers of believing that no matter where you are, happiness can be constant if you allow it.

Who you are is not what's happening outside of you. A stop sign on the road? Who cares? You're on a different path. You're standing up for who you are and who you are becoming. Nothing's going to stop that.

Patience is an opportunity to check in with the free-flowing inner journey of YOU. Can every day be an adventure, no matter where you are and what you're doing? Say YES!

Your Turn

STOP #16

VIEW *from the* SCENIC OVERLOOK

LOOK OUT at your future. Stop. Sit. Take a moment to do nothing. Consider, what if every morning you woke up feeling braver? Ready to activate adventure, no matter what comes your way. What would that feel like?

SHIFT GEARS: Can the strength of that joyful idea be patient? Can it endure an occasional "hold" in the midst of what's happening all around you? What will you say to yourself to keep your vision active?

EMERGENCY BRAKE: I'm overwhelmed. I'm too busy.

COMPASS CHECK-IN: Dream alive no matter what? or Dream stopped.

Now consider: How do I feel if I do? How do I feel if I don't?

Yes? No? Is it a GO?

BRAVE TRAVEL TIP: Roadblocks build patience.

NEXT:
I need my phone!

17

Is This a Movie?

The New Lens of Living

LIGHTS, CAMERA, ACTION. Driving down the Ventura highway, it felt like we were in a movie. We watched surfers and stopped to visit the sea lions who showed off their barks, grunts, and growls as they tumbled over each other, and generally hung out as a group. Interaction is always interesting to watch especially when you're looking at all the tourists taking selfies and photos everywhere. Were photos more important than the experience? Is "I was here," more important than being there?

I was used to pulling back from social media on this trip because Travis didn't believe in disturbing the experience. He had a flip phone! I, on the other hand, had my new phone with a good camera. Since I was trying out my new *Bravery Becomes You* Instagram story, I needed photos. And while it's now easy, at the time I was intimidated about expressing myself to the public. I had never said more than "happy birthday" on Facebook. But now, I was serious about my photo taking. The visual story of my brave journey was an essential part of my business plan, which I wanted to share as a coach, speaker, and author. I didn't want to just tell people how and why to be brave, I wanted to walk the talk as I tested my theory that bravery is the antidote to fear.

Frankly, I was afraid of technology. I felt challenged, inept, and frustrated every time I tried something new. This time, the challenge was posting on Instagram and Facebook. So day after day, I had been slowly getting over my insecurity, but it still took me a ridiculous amount of time to think of what I wanted to say, overanalyze it, and post it with a photo. It was time-consuming. It was also frustrating because often there was no internet service. Grabbing an opportunity to go through my painfully slow "put myself out there" story wasn't easy. But I was loving it. I enjoyed being heard. Getting a response. (Although one of my friends asked why I wasn't posting anything, and I discovered that I was sending the information to my personal, not bravery site.) Technology challenged? Oh, yeah.

For the most part, Travis was supportive, but not patient. He didn't like driving with someone staring at a phone. I agree. I don't like that either. On the other hand, I didn't have anywhere else but the car. And we were together 24 hours a day!!! It all worked out, but it was one thing we weren't in sync about. Of course, I took photos. We took photos of each other. We did some selfies. All was good.

We checked out Malibu, although you can't see much of the beach through the "wall" of homes. It's been claimed! We arrived at Venice beach and met one of Travis's friends. Lots to look at here! This eccentric, quirky and creative scene was another visual treat filled with skateboarders, colorful vendors, drum circles, street art, and muscle enthusiasts. And a "must do" for me? My first ever swim in the Pacific.

Time to leave. Bye, West Coast.

GETTING BRAVER—WHAT I LEARNED ABOUT FEAR: *I can put down my phone.*

So you ask, what does *that* have to do with fear? What does that have to do with your future vision? A lot. I've noticed that I turn to my phone for all kinds of reasons. I'm curious. I'm looking for information. I'm checking in to see what people I know are doing, and I'm using my camera…and on and on. All that is good, but I know the truth, and I like to ignore it. My phone is my procrastination, my worry, my anxiety, my answer to whatever is bothering me. My phone is one giant distraction, and it works for everything I don't want to deal with.

I'm including this subject here because time is valuable. I'm sure you know you probably spend a lot of time on social media. If you don't, then you deserve congratulations.

But, reality check? This is a habit that's stealing your future.

It's also doing something more. It alters the beauty of and emotional power of experience. Instead of looking up and out and noticing the amazing world right in front of you, you're busy elsewhere. You're not living your story.

The answer? Balance and awareness. For me, seeing the Pacific Ocean for the first time required a photograph. And once I did that I changed the focus to just me and the sea. Taking it all in. Being part of the world. Creating memories that become part of your internal landscape affects who you are. There's a big difference between participating in life, not just saying I was there in a picture. Being there is what gives life meaning.

And bravery? It's not easy to put down that phone. It's a strong, persistent, and distracting habit. Technology is always there, but your future is waiting too.

Your Turn

STOP #17

VIEW *from the* SCENIC OVERLOOK

LOOKING OUT at your precious future, consider the distraction of social media. How much time does it waste in your day? What do you use it for?

SHIFT GEARS: I'd like to use social media for good reasons. I can do that. I like that. What will you do?

EMERGENCY BRAKE: Forget it. I can't break the habit. What if there's a text?

COMPASS CHECK-IN: See your life in pictures? or In person?

Now consider: How do I feel if I do? How do I feel if I don't?

Yes? No? Is it a GO?

BRAVE TRAVEL TIP: Don't miss the view that's right in front of you!

NEXT:
Listening to fear.

18

You Want Me To Step Where?

Start with a Toe In?

"I CAN'T DO IT." We were on our way to see a very special swimming hole in Fish Camp, California. I thought we'd just have to walk down a nice path, and there we'd be. Wrong. First problem? Trying to figure out how I could possibly walk over a waterfall that we had to cross first. Followed by the confusing thought, "Why is there always an impossible challenge in front of me!" Answered with hope, "What could be better for a Bravery Becomes You test of strength!"

Nice try. Forget all that internal problem-solving. My scared/danger meter said this is serious stuff. "Why?" I shouted to the trees. Travis stood patiently on the other side of the rocks I needed to cross. He'd had absolutely no problem getting there. Not me. The rocks were slippery, and if I slipped I would have taken a tumbling ride through a waterfall. The end wouldn't have been a nice one. I hated to admit that my faulty knees made scrambling over anything an unsteady proposition. I didn't like this at all. I hadn't given up, but I was close.

I'd tested the rocks with the toe of my sneaker. "No way," I said. Then I took my shoes off. "No way!" I said again. I think I was talking to myself, offering encouraging ideas. But nothing seemed to be getting past my wish to live through this. And then? I spoke those awful words, "I can't do this.

I'm not going to do this. I give up. There is no chance I'm crossing this, and we've got to go back." This was my first "turn back" moment, and it didn't feel good. I wanted to do this. I was looking forward to the swimming holes that I'd heard so much about. I stood frozen with my decision. And then? I remembered I had a pair of water shoes in my backpack. "Okay. One more try." I slipped them on and tested the rocks again. There was just enough grip. So maybe I could do this. And I did. "I'm here!" I announced proudly to Travis who had been very calm and nice as he listened to my endless problem solving and worry. I think he was just glad not to turn back. We continued our trek down through a muddy, slippery path and except for a few awkward places to climb down, we arrived.

Three beautiful pools of water, in the middle of nowhere, on a hot summer day, was a perfect gift. And we were the only ones there. All ours.

One problem? It was unbelievably cold. Really? Another obstacle? In the past, I would have said, "This is nice, I'll just put my feet in the water, you go in." But this was a once-in-a-lifetime moment and (...new thought...) I'd never be here again. I put my toe in to test the chill. It wasn't just cold, it was "take your breath away" cold.

Should I do it? Perfect time for my inner compass. I closed my eyes. "How do I feel if I do? How do I feel if I don't?" I asked.

I imagined leaving. I saw myself waiting while Travis swam. Maybe crossing the waterfall was enough bravery for me. This was a disappointing scenario. And if I went in? I didn't know what would happen. But did I want to miss the joy of being brave, trying something new, and pushing myself? I'd never have another chance. The decision was clear.

"I'm going in," I said joyfully. "But let me figure out how!" There was a ledge of white rock that appeared to have a rough surface, surrounding the first pool. My method? Well... I was petrified of getting into the water too fast. I wasn't sure how I'd handle the shock of cold, (I'm used to cold Atlantic water, but this was far colder) so I devised my own brilliant method. I sat and slid, and slid, and slid against the scratchy surface. I had to cross about six feet of rock. It wasn't pleasant. There were also tiny bees everywhere. I'm not fond of being stung either. If anyone was watching, this wasn't a pretty picture.

But now I was determined. I made it to the edge. One toe in. Then one foot. Then another. Step by step...Wow. Then standing. Going lower. And lower. Until yes yes yes. I was in! This was the coldest water ever, but I was going to survive. I did it. I stood up and enjoyed the warm blanket of sun.

"That's just pool one," said Travis.

I probably rolled my eyes at this point. "Okay, do I really need to do this again? I'm proud of myself. I pushed myself. Water is water, right?"

"You have to do all three," said Travis. "That's part of the experience. It's great. Come on."

Pool two was okay. No full immersion shock. Now pool three. "There's a slide right here that takes you from two to three," Travis said. "It's easy." A slide? That means no control over how fast I get in the water.

So, once again. "I need time to figure this out." I sat on the top rocks and edged myself carefully, very carefully down the slide made of...you guessed it...slippery rocks. And I was in. But now I had to laugh. I'm still laughing. I'd imagined a big slide...maybe the size of a playground slide. This slide? It was about 3 feet long. It was nothing. I had made such a big deal out of nothing. It was a baby slide. Or barely a slide.

Lesson learned. I remembered again that fears are not facts. I loved that I was wrong. That this was silly. I'd made such a big deal out of nothing. Mission accomplished. Compass reliable.

And then we had to walk back. UP.

Now I was bold. Proud. Thrilled with my accomplishment. Joyful at the amazing experience of not just visiting these treasured pools but going in all three. I was in a special place that most people don't even know about. Yay me!

Time to leave, but it was an uphill climb. UP AND UP. Slippery, muddy up.

Mud is like ice. It's not easy to grip. So grabbing onto branches and jamming your feet into rocks for leverage worked best. Then I came to the spot I'd had some trouble with on the way down. It was too high for me to climb up. I tried a few awkward attempts but my legs weren't long enough. I needed help. So Travis went first, grabbed my hand, I grabbed a tree limb and success!

But now I had a gash on my leg and blood was dripping down. Did I care? No. I was so proud of myself. I can only imagine what I looked like after a chilly swim, wet and soggy, with blood dripping down my leg. But as we passed a group of people on their way down, they asked with great concern, "Are you okay?"

"I'm great," I said with enthusiastic confidence. As I passed them, I offered my newly confident "bit of bragging" advice. "The water is great. It's worth going in. You'll get used to the cold." Wise me!

GETTING BRAVER—WHAT I LEARNED ABOUT FEAR: *Saying YES feels wonderful when it feels right...for me.*

This day was a turning point moment. I'd been uncomfortable, uncertain, and scared over and over, but now I was facing physical limitations. I wasn't always sure what was safe for me or even possible. If my knees didn't work right, if my balance was a little off, if I simply didn't have the strength, then I'd have to face that.

It's disheartening to feel the twinges of "I'm different because of my age." I don't mind being realistic, but I also don't have to let that stop me if I don't want it to. On this occasion, I also realized that in the past, I often didn't try if something seemed "too much." There's always a reason you can talk yourself out of something. It doesn't matter at what stage of life you are.

What matters is that you check-in and find out what you *really* want to do! And what was I finding out? I'm getting braver. I want to be brave more than anything. I don't want to sit on the sidelines. I want to push myself. This story wasn't about physical limitations, this was, "What do I want to do about it?"...With a capital I.

But whatever I do, I also want to do it my way. And that's why the *Get Brave Compass* works so well. Bringing your attention back to the moment and considering how you feel (not what you think), makes every choice the right choice. For YOU.

Putting how you feel on hold, happens. Sometimes it has to. But now, "How do I feel?" has a nice ring to it. Don't you think?

And if you need some extra help doing what you want to do, then ask for a hand to pull you up!

Your Turn

STOP #18

VIEW *from the*
SCENIC OVERLOOK

LOOKING OUT at your exciting future, close your eyes, and see yourself energized and happy. Pay close attention to how you feel. Now choose something you really think you want, and check to see if it's a match to the emotions you just enjoyed. What did you choose? Why?

SHIFT GEARS: What step could you take to move forward? Do you need help? Who would you ask? Write down your ideas.

EMERGENCY BRAKE: I don't trust my feelings.

COMPASS CHECK-IN: I make decisions by thinking only or I do both. But I feel first and think second.

Now consider: How do I feel if I do? How do I feel if I don't?

Yes? No? Is it a GO?

BRAVE TRAVEL TIP: The best direction is one feeling away.

NEXT:
Wrinkles everywhere.

19

Wizened Beauty?

A Lovely Wrinkle

"OLD IS BEAUTIFUL!" I'm so ready to embrace that as my mantra of aging. Images of perfection, usually based on a standard of "young," do nothing for self-esteem no matter what age you are. So far on my mostly mirrorless journey, combined with my image of myself as the "mom" traveling with her son, gave me an instant boost of youthful "Keeping up with Travis" energy. I felt a glow of liking myself in a new way. Inner, invisible beauty from confidence was putting my traditional beauty standards on hold. Was bravery beautiful?

I lost track of how I looked on the outside most of the time. Although I couldn't escape my old habit of checking out my appearance in the somewhat distorted side view mirror. What a picture! Windswept and happy. But I was also facing the truth that I don't look the same as I used to. As self-protection, I always try to push those thoughts away. Aging gracefully is the nice thing to say. But those lines!!! They linger in my mind. Darn.

It's clear to me that, in general, society doesn't embrace the wise beauty of years gone by. Wrinkles of wisdom aren't treasured. And for me, looking good is an ingrained habit that I can't totally toss aside. I could compromise and get used to a new me, but shallow as it may seem, what experience feels good if you think you don't look good? It was something I faced every morning as I crawled out of the tent without my typical morning ritual of "getting ready" and putting on "my best face." Now I grabbed my prepacked "get ready in the morning bag," retrieved my toothbrush, poured water in a cup, and brushed my teeth. Oh bliss! Baby wipes (unscented) for a general dusting off and makeup wipes to wash my face. I brushed my hair and that was it. This was different for me. When we first began our journey, I used the visor mirror in the car to add a little eyeliner. That was the least I could do, right? When I thought about it, I knew that at home, I never ever went out without makeup. That was a firm rule in my beauty book. But now, weeks later, I didn't even do that. Fearless liberation? It felt that way, and it was. And my hair? Well...occasional showers, interspersed with swimming became "my look." Best of all, I didn't care. I was fine. I survived. People still talked to me and liked me. I was not my mascara and eyeliner, I was me. (Sounds crazy, right?) I'd lived the message that often runs through a woman's life – "If you want to be happy, confident, and successful, you have to play by society's beauty standards." Wrong!

I now knew better. It's bravery that makes you confident, and nothing looks better than that. Bravery was my best shade of foundation!

So when we arrived at the Bristlecone Pines site in Great Basin National Park and met the longest living trees in the world, I felt transformed by the message of their survival. These twisted, gnarled, weathered, barely looking alive pines are like works of art. The oldest, most decimated ones are the true winners, as they live in the harshest, worst, windiest conditions. Younger trees, which face more comfortable weather and land conditions, grow faster and look better, but they don't live as long. Thriving in adversity is the law of beauty here, and some of these trees are thousands of years old.

Gnarled into patterns of dark and white, standing bent and bare, I felt a connection to these treasures that spoke a silent truth. "Aging is a beautiful thing."

Gone was the usual message—"You're not good enough, don't look good enough, aren't wise enough." The replacement? "Wrinkles, lines, and all that goes with getting older are signs of resilience, strength, surviving, and thriving."

This was a bravery metaphor moment. The beauty of your own unique story, the one that will stand the test of time, is the tale of how, against the odds, you pushed through. No matter the outcome, you were brave enough to try and keep trying. Being confident in your commitment to stand up for who you are and who you want to be, is the best story on earth. And I want that! I think we all do.

But still? Aging woes seem everywhere. I had to wonder, how aging would affect my present and future? After all, I'm not a tree. Was I going to be scared because there's ageism in the job market and the fashion magazines? There are wrinkles on my face? My motivation and energy are changing in ways that I don't always understand? Life after 50 is an adjustment to a new way of living and being. There's an opportunity to enjoy a new mindset energized by an endpoint that wasn't as clear before. But confusion and trepidation are tangled into those concepts. My friends, coaching clients, and warnings that abound in social media are telling me so.

But really! Aging doesn't need to include fear as an adjective when it's a process that results in mature beauty that reflects strength, power, and wisdom. It's time for a new story and the opportunity to let go of what we should do. Adventure is waiting. Not ending.

GETTING BRAVER—WHAT I LEARNED ABOUT FEAR: *I am not my eyeliner.*

Letting go of how I thought I should look didn't change the way anyone related to me. I still had the same kind of conversations, the same fun, the same adventure, the same problems, no matter the shape or condition of my image. In fact, most of the time on this trip, I completely forgot about what I must look like. There was the occasional, "I'm out in public and I forgot to brush my hair" shock, but for the first time in a long time, that didn't bother me. Once I forgot to think about "what I'm wearing, and how I'm looking," the focus of the subject disappeared.

I also thought about the message of the trees. The ones that had withstood the most adversity and looked barely alive were the strong ones. They had a story to tell and that fascinated me as I stood in awe before them. It made me think that it's time to change the "negative" aging look, to a look that's appreciated, that shows off a life well-lived, that's stood the test of time and survived. To be honored as sages and seen with a confident beauty all our own. Wouldn't that be nice!

And the beauty secret we can all enjoy? When *Bravery Becomes You*, confidence happens. And nothing is more becoming than confidence.

Your Turn

STOP #19

VIEW from the SCENIC OVERLOOK

LOOKING OUT at your precious future, consider your life experience. See yourself as a sage with wisdom to share. What are three truths about life you'd offer to someone younger (say 24 years old, like my son!).

SHIFT GEARS: Aging is beautiful. What makes your confidence shine?

EMERGENCY BRAKE: Aging is not a good look.

COMPASS CHECK-IN: I like the person in the mirror inside and out or If I looked different, I'd be happier.

Now consider: How do I feel if I do? How do I feel if I don't?

Yes? No? Is it a GO?

BRAVE TRAVEL TIP: It's never too late to be YOU.

Time to write!

NEXT:
Ewwwwwww.

20

When "Ewwwww" is Okay

Sharing is Caring

HERE'S ANOTHER "if you could only see us now" moment. As it was every day, there we were, mother and son, singing Grateful Dead songs (which at some point I knew by heart), eating gummy bears, checking out the atlas of maps (I loved that book), and sharing a water bottle! Yes, sharing a water bottle. Sound disgusting? It might have been at some point. (I don't generally share a water bottle at home but it's amazing what you get used to).

Like many things you wouldn't think you'd like, I forgot about germs and became very fond of that big white, kind of dirty looking, covered with stickers plastic bottle leftover from Travis's college years. I also don't know why we didn't have our own water bottles. Maybe there was no room. The car was jammed full of pillows and blankets, clothes drying that I'd washed out in some sink, bags of camping stuff, well-worn pamphlets, maps, bags of what I thought were organized "what you'll need to go swimming or hiking gear," and an amazing pile of junk that seemed to accumulate at my feet. "No more room," I'd quickly and defensively say when Travis tried to add something to my side on the floor. There was also my notebook where I jotted down locations and memories to use someday in my book!!!

But whatever the reason, germs and all, we shared that bottle. A lot. Water is serious business when you discover the meaning of DRY!!! Growing up on the East Coast, I'd never thought anything much about water except "drink eight glasses a day," which I didn't do, but knew I should. It didn't have much impact.

Out West? Drinking water is a non-negotiable activity. You need to drink it all the time. ALL THE TIME!!! You can never run out. Ever. And we never forgot to fill and refill our supply. Stop for gas. Fill up the water bottle. Stop for groceries. Fill up the bottle. Go on the hike? Fill up the water bottle. If you don't, you just might not make it back.

So the habit of water was constant. If Travis picked up the water and took a drink, he passed it to me. If I picked it up, I passed it to him. Same when hiking. When you took a break, everyone drank. Didn't matter if you wanted to. You never passed up the opportunity.

That water bottle was part of our journey. It was our peace pipe of sharing and caring that the other person was okay. If we were annoyed, we shared and drank water. If we were tired, we did the same. Drinking water offered a moment of checking in until we got back to being awestruck by the world going by our windows.

And checking in was essential when not enough water can lead to dehydration. Could it happen to us? One day it almost did.

It happened when we were traveling from the highest point in the USA to the lowest. We began at Mount Whitney, the tallest mountain in the contiguous United States with an elevation of 14,505 feet. Spectacular, of course. (I also appreciated the ever-present road signs that warned us that "this is active bear territory.") After seeing all things wonderful, we headed in the other direction to HOT. We were now on our way to Death Valley, the lowest point in the USA, at 300 feet below sea level. Was it getting hotter? Oh yes, hotter and hotter. At one point we discovered it was 117 degrees and the forecast was for even *hotter*. It didn't feel that bad, but there was a heaviness to the air and the added drama of the name Death Valley.

As the day continued, I began to notice the heat in a new way. Even with the windows rolled down and the wind whipping my hair around, I felt uncomfortable, and a little woozy. Now you're probably thinking, what about air conditioning? I was thinking that too. But not for us. According to Travis, having the engine work hard by using air conditioning wasn't good for the car. The car could overheat and then where would we be?

Hotter! Stranded on the side of the road. Not good. And even better? He turned on the heat, which cools the engine. Oh. Look what I'm learning! But what about all the other cars going by, windows rolled up? I could only imagine the cool inside. Oh well. I didn't understand what he said at first, but I had to agree. What he said sounded correct. We might have been hot in our car, but we knew what we were doing!

Time to be resourceful. I perched my leg out the window hoping that gravity was a cure for my swelling ankles. FYI...It feels good to hang your leg out the window!

We finally got to Badwater Basin, THE lowest spot in North America at 282 feet below sea level. Ready to get out of the car and walk? Of course. And I did. I appreciated the incredible views and the sign that marked the altitude. But as I started down the long walk into the basin's salt flats, I told Travis to go ahead without me. I was beginning to feel a bit weird. So off he went and I edged forward slowly and not too far. Being there, in this vast, flat, hot, scenic, desolate wonderland was something I liked. It was like being on another planet. Nothing familiar. Something new to take in. I always enjoy feeling my brain trying to figure life out. Although, right then, my brain was beginning to feel what I can only describe as "ditsy."

I could feel I was getting hotter. I had read some info that outlined the dangers of being overheated. I was experiencing some of the signs like feeling a little sick and not thinking clearly. Was I imagining all this? It seemed kind of silly. I'd been drinking water all day.

Back in the car, we headed to the visitor center which was about to close. Travis bought me a sports drink and I sipped gingerly as I watched the tourists buying tee-shirts and Death Valley souvenirs. Travis was busy as usual asking questions at the information center. He was probably asking what to do with his mother who was about to have a heat stroke!

This nice refuge was about to close, so we went outside, where I drank more than I thought possible from the water fountain.

And then I saw Travis coming toward me. He had our favorite water bottle in his hands. Was he about to fill it up? No. I could see it was full. He came closer. And then I instinctively knew exactly what he was going to do.

"Don't do that." I said firmly, "I mean it. Don't do that!" I said again.

Didn't matter. He took that bottle, raised it over my head, and poured the entire contents of freezing cold water...YES...over me. All over me!!!

I was shocked. I was sopping wet.

"Why? Why? Why? Travis!!!"

"You have to cool down," he said. "This is a good way to do it." And, "It's so hot, you'll dry off in a minute."

He was right. By the time I walked to the car, I not only felt a little better, I was almost dry.

He was taking care of me, and that was nice. Just a bit shocking!!!

GETTING BRAVER—WHAT I LEARNED ABOUT FEAR: *Sometimes "not good" is "good."*

There was another surprise for me on this day of contrasts. Going from the highest elevation to the lowest in a matter of hours made me think about the push/pull of right and wrong, good and bad, acceptable/not acceptable. I've definitely made up a lot of rules about what I like/don't like and...Oh no! Now I find out. There's no reason to follow them.

Thinking a little more flowed into the thought that there aren't just the 2 sides (pro and con) of any experience. There are infinite ways to interpret what's happening. Life isn't just about how I feel about a simple water bottle or a chilly shower; it's about handling an endless mix of emotions and daily actions. To make day-to-day life easy, I've created "automatic" solutions that don't require any decision-making. Action on default mode.

And that's fine when you know it's nice to say please and thank you, or that it's important to close the freezer door because things will melt, but set responses put limits on the infinite variety of options that are available.

But now? Who cares about what's acceptable or appropriate? Or right or wrong? I want to shake off old thinking and let in the new. And yet, how can I take new steps forward if I'm constantly avoiding my curious question "what's next?" by answering with predetermined, outdated words? As you've read in my other stories, the conflict of old and new is a recurring theme.

It's time to re-evaluate our thinking, one of the most important and productive first steps to take when a desire to change is on the horizon. Loosening the reins of autopilot answers opens the avenue of communication so you can get in touch with how you want to feel when you wake up in the morning. These are fresh-start moments that can make you receptive to things you haven't thought of yet. When you're ready to soar and have no idea what to do next or how to do what you want, you simply need a new way to think about all the endless possibilities while waiting for your YES.

For me, not relying on traditional yes/no solutions is a whole new outrageously exciting adventure that makes me feel a little ill at the same time. How can I venture into this new open-ended, "I can do anything" mode when I'm not sure I know what that means?

The answer I've found? Enjoy the journey. Love the process of unraveling what's old. Make it a pleasure to learn new ways of being yourself. Let go and wander within to hear your own voice that's longing to grow. Consider different options for living a life that has meaning for YOU.

I think of this as decluttering, cleaning out your closet, down-sizing. Getting rid of what you don't need is liberating. Get rid of the old. Let in the new.

And how do you do that? Wake up as the brave adventurer delighted to challenge the past and the many rules you live by.

Amuse yourself. Play with your everyday patterns. Breakfast for dinner. Dessert first. Go to the movies in the morning, or go alone. Read a genre of book that you always said you didn't like but you've never tried. Draw a picture, even if you've always said you're not good at art. And guess what? No one is watching but you. No one is judging but you. The rules only exist because you've decided they exist. Shake it up! See what happens.

You can try the "what's acceptable" game. A new skill? Yes. Having fun, letting go, and getting rid of the rules. Yes. Wait, what??? Yes, you can do this too. Rules aren't fun, they're rigid. Not creative. And you're moving toward flexibility, right? So try "guidelines." Create them. Change them. They're scaffolding that supports you but doesn't restrict you.

And what's unacceptable? Change careers at 50? Move to a new country at 55? Skydive at 60? Start a business at 65? Find love at 70? Keep working until 80? Do you have ideas about what you can't do because of your age? Are you concerned about what other people believe?

It's time to lose your old definitions of what's acceptable and appreciate "restriction-free" experiments in living.

Drinking out of the same water bottle? Unacceptable. Until it was. Using a water bottle to extinguish an overheated mother? Well…he did it, didn't he? And it was a good thing!

Who says you can't get a job at 80 or become an artist at 60? Who says?

It's time to give old ideas the cold shoulder and appreciate the many sides of experience.

No ice cold water required!

Your Turn

STOP #20

VIEW *from the* SCENIC OVERLOOK

LOOKING OUT at your precious future, see how decluttering your list of rules would change your path forward. What would you like to let go of that is in your way?

SHIFT GEARS: What will you do now, that you didn't do before. List some actions you'll take.

EMERGENCY BRAKE: I love rules.

COMPASS CHECK-IN: Release old rules? or Keep them?

Now consider: How do I feel if I do? How do I feel if I don't?

Yes? No? Is it a GO?

BRAVE TRAVEL TIP: Acceptable isn't a rule! You can break it.

NEXT:
I'm Scared

21

Driving with One Eye Open

Can I Cry Now?

"YOU'RE GETTING TOO CLOSE!!!" I tried to say calmly, the edge of a scream sitting on the tip of my tongue. We'd been on this mountain road for a while, but as we climbed higher, the level of my rising fear was a perfect match to our altitude. I was having a silent conversation with myself that was a continuous mantra of "please please please, let's not go over the edge," combined with "lots of people drive up these roads and are okay." As I looked out my window, the depth of our impending fall drew mental pictures and plans about how we'd survive. Could I jump out of the car and grab onto a tree?

The crumbling edge of the road crept closer and closer. From my side of the car, I had a clear view of the "do not cross" white line that was eroded or in places, totally gone. It was impossible not to sound like the critical mom I was hoping I left at home. A shrill "this is your mother speaking" request to "please drive toward the center of the road" was said with a tone of urgency and pending death hysteria in my voice.

I got a quick response back. "I know what I'm doing," said Travis. "What do you think? I want to die?" Well, he had a point. But he also had no idea what it looked like outside my window. I know I've said I'm getting used to trusting Travis. And I believe he has an uncanny knack for being careful and making good decisions. But what could he do if this was the moment when the road collapsed? What was a mother to do? Gripping the seat did nothing. Leaning toward the left wasn't going to keep the car from falling to the right. There was nothing left to say.

The only thing I could come up with? Close one eye and squint out of the other. I could still keep my "back seat driver" mind on the road while blocking my view of the deepening drop on my side. At this point, the car was rocking over the rocks we were crossing, and they were getting bigger and bigger. Travis actually got out of the car to move some of them. Uncomfortable doesn't describe it! Forget my brilliant one-eye closed solution. I was holding on for life! I needed all my senses on high alert, so I could shout what I knew would be pointless orders to slow down or turn back. And then it got worse!

"This can't be happening!" On the road ahead, which had only gotten narrower and narrower, a car appeared from around a corner. "They've just got to back up," I announced firmly. Well that wasn't going to happen, and we certainly couldn't go in reverse. We couldn't even turn around. Changing direction was impossible. We were going forward no matter what. The car kept coming toward us, nearer and nearer, until their bumper was inches from ours. A dance of danger was happening as each car kept inching carefully forward, somehow finding a sliver of space to pass by. But to make that space, our car was right on...yes...the edge. Closer and closer. That crumbling white line was under our tires. This was serious to me. I was gripping the door. Sitting straight up. My heart was pounding in a different beat from the music that was always playing. And again, I was powerless.

Nothing to do. No answer. No safety net. No good brainstorming solutions.

And so I did what any intelligent person would do. I started to cry. "I can't bear to watch this."

"Then don't," said Travis. Stunned with the simplicity of the solution, I closed my eyes, shut out the danger. And survived. This wasn't the last time I would cry.

GETTING BRAVER—WHAT I LEARNED ABOUT FEAR: *Boundaries matter.*

Like now, when the idea of plunging down a ravine wasn't a good thought. But was I giving anguish a free pass to repeat? Sure this was scary. Yes, I needed to see if there was a way to change what was happening. Yes, I needed to process my concern and face it. But did I need to be stuck in a broken record of, "What if something bad happens?" No. I didn't have to keep making myself feel worse.

And yes, I've done that many times in my life when that loop of dealing with something that rocked my sense of self or that made me afraid that my life was changing in some way I didn't like, kept me in a state of unease. And I know I am very capable of keeping that worry on a steady cycle of repeat!

But now, I know better. When something shakes my world, I give myself permission to mull it over. But only up to a point. When I find myself rehashing the same idea again and again, making myself feel bad again and again, keeping myself agitated and unproductive as I wait to "get over it," I put up a stop sign.

Setting a time limit for worry? A boundary for fear? It works. It makes me feel good. It means I'm taking care of myself.

Wow. Amazing what I learned in a car ride of fear!

(And FYI—even when you take control of how long you will stay in a place of fear or worry, it doesn't mean it won't keep popping up. So when it does, notice it, give it a little time, and then say a gentle, but firm, "enough.")

Worry is also a tricky fear. It's not always linked to a specific event. It lives in the daily musings of, "What do I do next? What if I don't know what I want my future to be? What if I never change?"

That worry/fear loop is diverting your attention from your dreams, damaging the quality of your day, and keeping you stuck.

The real question? How much time do you have to give this negative force? Is all that thinking getting in the way of doing what you truly want to do?

❧

Your Turn

STOP #21

VIEW *from the*
SCENIC OVERLOOK

LOOKING OUT at your beautiful future, imagine joy, and then add worry. Does it fit? What worries do you want to leave behind?

SHIFT GEARS: Can you say "ENOUGH!" to those worry loops? Choose one of your most persistent worries. Write it down and then write "ENOUGH."

EMERGENCY BRAKE: I'm a worrier. I can't change.

COMPASS CHECK-IN: Worry rules your day? or You rule your day?

Now consider: How do I feel if I do? How do I feel if I don't?

Yes? No? Is it a GO?

BRAVE TRAVEL TIP: The road to worry leads nowhere.

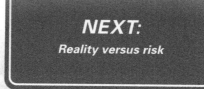

NEXT:
Reality versus risk

22

How Far We've Come

Taking a Chance

"I'M IN LOVE."

Now that we've spent weeks in Oregon, Washington, Nevada, and California, we're on the road to the Grand Staircase experience in Utah. Capitol Reef, Bryce Canyon, and Zion National Parks are about to stretch my vision like never before. Postcards of raw beauty that are out of this world!

I loved it all, but this story begins with our last stop of the day. Zion. We were planning to hike up the famed Narrows, a gorge where, if you choose, you walk up the narrow Virgin River. After negotiating the parking lot (many visitors!), I needed to put on my bathing suit, in the car. I was trying to be discreet, wrestling with my suit in the dripping hot heat of the Utah sun. Miserable. Amazing how angry you can get putting on a bathing suit.

Next? A clearly marked sign said, "Flood Level—RISKY" at the Narrows (the place I wanted to go most!). Justified worry? Yes. In fact, in 2015, seven people were swept away and died due to storm flooding. Flash floods are deceiving. The sun can be out, the sky blue, and with lightning speed, a flood can arrive from somewhere else. Oh dear!

So, we asked the rangers. Their response? "Go at your own risk." Since it was bright and sunny, we got on the required bus transportation and arrived at the Narrows with lots and lots of people, all heading for the canyon. Like lemmings (who follow one another off a cliff to their deaths), we went too.

It was strange trying to gauge if this was okay. My normal senses weren't working. I didn't want to disappoint myself. Everyone's going, right? It must be okay. The rangers are letting people go, and I'd previewed this hike at home on TV. I was ready. We decided to take a careful risk (not sure how you really do that). Rationalization? You bet! Stupid? Probably.

The water was murky and brown (it's usually clear) and it was much higher than normal, and getting higher as we made our way slowly over the incredibly slippery rocks under our feet. Visibility? Zero. We couldn't see where to step next, and the rocks weren't steady. Each inch forward took a lot of exploration with our toes to find a solid spot. Twisting an ankle was not unlikely. Luckily, I'd brought my hiking poles, so with awkward maneuvering (kind of like I had four arms), we headed in.

No question, it was amazing. The rock formations. The red walls. The raw force of nature was transforming. But the entire time, I was thinking about floods. I was monitoring the water, and after about an hour we both agreed that the water was getting too high. It was time to turn back and go one hour the other way. Of course, all of this was not very smart. If there was going to be a flash flood, a few inches of water rising wasn't the predictor. We thought we were being careful, but what kind of nature savvy was that?

Amazing what you'll do when you want something! Weighing the risks. Taking a chance. This time the decision was right. Next time, who knows? But who cares? We got back to the car. And now? It was time to figure out where to eat and sleep.

At the grocery store, we listened to all the tourists talking about staying in the campgrounds or the hotels that lined the road into the park. Well, that wasn't for us (though it did sound kind of nice).

Of course, I was feeling vulnerable, but Travis already knew what he wanted to find. He had a spot picked out. He'd been there before, but couldn't remember exactly where! Great! Could I try to sit back and relax? Only worry a little? Oh progress!!!

And then...this sounded *very* iffy. "This is the best spot in Zion and most people think they can't go there," explained Travis. "You have to cross a 20-foot piece of road that has a clear 'No Trespassing' sign. Within minutes, there's another road, and then a little way up the road, there's a sign that makes it clear that this is public land."

This made absolutely no sense. How do you get there, when you have to break the law? I found out. You just do it.

And we did. We found the correct turnoff and there was the No Trespassing sign. And then, just across the way, was the next road we needed to take (at least Travis was *pretty* sure at this point). Up up, up we drove. And when we reached the top? Wow again. We were overlooking Zion. We would be sleeping in the best place you can imagine, cradled in red canyon majesty. It was perfect, except for one thing.

Thunderstorms! We had checked the forecast throughout the day, and now it had changed. A storm was coming right at us. The possibility of a lightning strike on our very exposed, very high perch didn't make it sound like a comfortable place for sweet dreams. What's more, if it rained, the red sandstone road we'd driven up would most likely turn into a slick river. Our drive down would be impossible. We would be stuck.

What a day! Flash floods and lightning and roads that dissolve into mud. Hmmm. Heart-pounding fun? I wasn't sure. I wasn't used to spending so much time trying to decide if I was safe. Would I wake up in the morning? Would I be stranded? Would we be electrocuted by white-hot bolts from the sky? There we were weighing the risks and making educated (as best we could) decisions. We were in charge of us, but not nature. There was a big IF in our evening.

We were creating the future step by step, and that included taking chances. We decided to wait and check the weather later. We set everything up, ate our dinner overlooking the vista of Zion, and then checked the radar again. The storm had changed direction and was not coming toward our amazing spot. We knew that could change. Didn't matter. We made a decision. Time to sleep and wake up to tomorrow's thrill ride. A new skill set: negotiating fear. Wow, this is fun!!!!

GETTING BRAVER—WHAT I LEARNED ABOUT FEAR: *Sometimes your heart needs a lawyer!*

So far on this trip, I'd counted on my always reliable *Get Brave Compass*. It was becoming clear that checking in with my feelings made it easier to cut through the emotional clutter of old habits, and instead come up with new answers that are aligned with what's best for me.

But what if your feelings are tied? What wins? The answer is YOU. No matter what comes your way... flash floods, lightning, unexpected new responsibilities, or demands from others' expectations of what you need to do, you can still retain top priority status. And why would you do something if your heart's not in it?

Time for some risk analysis. First, no question, there are times when you need to step outside of your plans and respect what needs to be done whether it's for personal or business reasons. There are so many things that ask for your attention: work issues, other people's problems, family needs, taking care of finances, cooking dinner!...Diversions are everywhere. All the time! But knowing your value also means finding a new way to make decisions about YOU. It means ditching distraction and the old habits of unintentionally giving away your energy to people, projects, and crises that will always be there. Often your heart is pulled in two directions. But still? Don't forget you, no matter what's going on.

And when other things start to take over, a *View from the Scenic Overlook* is the perfect bravery tool. Wherever you are, you can close your eyes, travel to the future, and enjoy the emotions that are revealed in your satisfying future. Nothing needs to make your vision fade. You're still part of whatever decision you make.

The key is to see the truth. Do you want to make "tomorrow" the mantra of your future? It doesn't have to be that way if you're willing to be brave. You can handle whatever comes your way and still activate your dreams IF you just decide that YOU won't be the last thing you consider.

So, can you take a chance on you?

You can do it by shifting your mindset. If something difficult happens, speak up. Negotiate your time and effort. Express your need for self-care, and yes...comfort! You are in charge of your happiness. It may take some extra courage to make it all work, but that's what bravery's for, right?

By changing your response to the world around you, you'll discover that you can do what you need to do and still do what you *want* to do. In the past it was easy to put yourself last, but loving yourself is important. By being brave again and again and using the *Get Brave Compass* as your guide, you'll eventually know how to face the future calmly and confidently, despite interference. It just takes practice.

The beauty of my road trip was that it allowed me to step away from the habits and responsibilities of my life and focus on what was right in front of me. And what happened? I was living a new way, free to experience each moment side by side with worry and fear that were tampering with my happiness. And once I woke up my confidence, I knew I could handle joy as well as conflict. I didn't need to be in the middle, negotiating what to feel or break a tie decision. I was in charge!

Bravery would eventually make life's everyday conflicts more manageable. Whatever needed to be done just fit in with my dreams. And that was doable!

So what about you? Are you your #1 priority? Are you worth the risk?

Your Turn

VIEW *from the* SCENIC OVERLOOK

LOOKING OUT at your wonderful future, imagine making your dreams a top priority. What encouragement would you give yourself about navigating the risks of distraction or unexpected responsibility? Write some wise words to yourself.

SHIFT GEARS: What action can you take no matter what's happening (it can be small)? Name one.

EMERGENCY BRAKE: What I want isn't that important.

COMPASS CHECK-IN: Take care of yourself? or Let distraction be your guide?

Now consider: How do I feel if I do? How do I feel if I don't?

Yes? No? Is it a GO?

BRAVE TRAVEL TIP: The risk is not taking the risk.

NEXT:
Is the story over?

23

Take me to the airport, I want to go home

Enough!

"I'VE HAD ENOUGH," I SAID with rage. I'm sure Travis had too. We were disagreeing about what direction to go and how long to stay at our next location. This was a conversation roadblock. No way around it. We were both "out of proportion" angry and probably about a lot more than this moment. Considering we had been together 24 hours a day with no break, it was amazing we were talking at all. We were in sync before this. Or were we?

"Take me to the airport, I want to go home," was my battle cry. I was done. Over it. Couldn't take another minute. I meant the words.

When I thought about it, we had many things we disagreed about. Most of it was little stuff. Like, I wanted coffee first thing in the morning. Travis didn't. He was in no rush and thought it was an addiction he was helping me get over. (Hmmm...) I didn't like that one bit. I had to tell him that if I seemed snippy, it was a sign I needed and wanted coffee. Addiction or not, I was going to be "out of sorts" without my coffee. Did he really want that? No, he didn't. And he wasn't my boss!!! And so, the coffee problem was solved.

Another issue was my new commitment to Instagram posts (which I mentioned earlier). It was something I was insecure about, and he didn't like it when I took a lot of time paying attention to the phone and not the view outside. He didn't want to be in a car with someone looking at a phone. We disagreed!!!

He was also adamant about checking out EVERYTHING. While I was always glad we followed his lead, he often didn't ask if that's what I wanted.

Many more little details bothered us differently. It was like, "who left the cap off the toothpaste?" small stuff. But these endless things were adding up.

And side by side for 24 hours a day? Let's consider that. At the time of this particular argument (yes, we had others), we had been on the road for 3 weeks. We were in the car for countless hours. We had to find places to eat and sleep, and determining which direction to go took some negotiation. Lots of decisions were made without knowing if the outcome would be positive. Where to have dinner was always a challenge. Yelp helped. The internet helped too, but it often wasn't available. Decisions included agreeing and disagreeing, and that meant someone had to give in!

Yet this argument seemed bigger than the others. As we drove, I fumed. I also mourned. Because if I actually went to the airport, our journey was over. The more I thought about that, the more I didn't want it to end.

I wanted a new story. I needed a new story. And now, I was *living* a new story. I was having one of the best experiences of my life. I was changing. Shifting. I was living *Bravery Becomes You,* and it worked. The more I was brave, the more I wanted to be brave. I looked forward to being brave. I couldn't wait to be brave. Bravery felt great. This from a confessed scaredy-cat?

That's when I woke up and realized that my *Bravery Becomes You* idea was what I wanted my life to be. It was clear. It's what I wanted to share with you. I wanted everyone to know the push/pull of change and the joy of crossing the threshold of resistance. It was exhilarating. I wanted to live this way for the rest of my life.

And now I was facing a real "walk the talk" moment. I was committed 100% to a new way of living. Bravery meant not compromising my YES!, and that also meant not letting any obstacles get in the way of the amazing life I was having at this very moment. Now, all I had to do was think and act in a new way, free from the old "shoulds" and rules of how things "ought to be." But could I?

What a perfect opportunity! A test to consider differences of opinion, perspectives, and whether or not someone else's behavior was going to influence me. Sifting through negative comments, different points of view, and variations on "what's acceptable" are a regular part of daily living. Someone (including me) is always there saying, "Are you sure you want to do this?" or "Do this tomorrow," or my father's favorite "What would you want to do that for?" I knew I wanted my brave quest to keep going, but, but, but…

Wait!!! Travis had something to say.

"I'm not your taxi driver," he sneered. I recoiled at his rude anger. But then he added, "I put a lot of work into figuring all this out and making sure it's good for you. I'm taking you to all the places I want you to see and experience."

My answer? "Well, why didn't you say so!"

He was resisting my directions because he thought I wasn't honoring all of his behind-the-scenes work. He always makes everything seem so effortless. I didn't know about his diligent preparation. I didn't realize how much he cared. Communication lesson for both of us. Don't assume you know what someone else is thinking!

But most of all, on this worst of days, I was experiencing the ultimate *Bravery Becomes You* moment. Having a difficult situation show up was perfect. It forced me to make my biggest decision yet.

Time for more bravery? Feeling uncomfortable, but able to move past that? Pushing myself over the threshold where the NOs were taunting me? Going for the golden opportunity?

How do I feel if I do? How do I feel if I don't? YES. NO. YES. NO…. YES!

I was confident this couldn't end. I didn't want it to. I loved the story I was living.

But moving forward wasn't just up to me. WE were at a bit of a stand-still. I now knew my son's perspective, and I couldn't figure out how we were going to get over this latest snag.

Luckily, with some silence and time, and our favorite Grateful Dead cassette (yes, it *was* a cassette!), we were heading down the highway, happy and committed to our amazing journey.

As we drove on, I flipped down the visor to see how I looked in the mirror. Was it true that there's nothing more attractive than confidence?

Well, without a shower or makeup, or even clean clothes, I'd have to rely on the confidence beauty philosophy while on the road. I liked what I saw. Grubby, kind of grimy, happy me.

GETTING BRAVER—WHAT I LEARNED ABOUT FEAR: *I direct my life story.*

Was I afraid of ending my trip? Oh, yeah. At this point, I was experiencing confidence like never before. I couldn't believe the satisfaction of pushing myself to be more, do more. The world felt like it was expanding around me.

Clarity that I didn't want this story to end, was also something new. I'm a waffling decision-maker. Knowing something without question felt good.

But this was more. This was about commitment. Letting go of anger. Letting go of being right. Letting go of how Travis should act and how I should respond. The only rule here was making this work. The bigger picture was what mattered most. We could do this!

And the biggest reason of all? I liked this new me. I did not want to return to "same old, same old" day-to-day living. This was showing me how to make the change I wanted real.

I knew I wanted bravery to motivate me, and to live free from confusion, indecision, doubt, and worry. This was an opportunity to see that in the next phase of my life, I could enjoy living life my way. Shaking off old patterns was showing me how possible this was. It was exhilarating.

Best of all, I didn't have to know where I was going or what I was going to do when I got there, I just had to be brave.

That's it. All I needed to navigate my future was bravery. I was set.

Your Turn

STOP #23

VIEW *from the*
SCENIC OVERLOOK

YOUR FUTURE looks clear when brave confidence energizes your actions. Rate your confidence right now on a scale from 1 to 10. Why did you choose this number?

SHIFT GEARS: What would it take to make it a 10? One brave step you could take?

EMERGENCY BRAKE: Confidence is overrated.

COMPASS CHECK-IN: I am brave or I'll never be brave.

NOW CONSIDER: How do I feel if I do? How do I feel if I don't?

Yes? No? Is it a GO?

BRAVE TRAVEL TIP: Confidence fuels my future.

NEXT:
*What happens if a giant
tree falls on you?*

24

We Could Have Died

Fear Doesn't Like Change

HOW NICE! WE WERE IN A BEAUTIFUL, comfortable campground. And yet? "Someone's throwing rocks." It was probably 2 a.m. when I heard a loud, clear, cracking sound that cut through the dark silence in our tent. Why would someone be out in the dark tossing rocks? That ever-present, vulnerable voice in my head whispered, "There's only tent fabric between everything scary and me," and mixed with that uncomfortable, heart-pounding adrenaline rush, I listened very carefully. Imagination? Animals? An angry person?

I waited in frozen silence, on high alert. Then it was quiet. There was no choice but to go back to sleep and wake up with the sun, curious about the nighttime rock thrower.

And in the morning? There was no evidence of anything unusual. The sound of the stream and the chatter of chipmunks was it. So much for my busy mind's storytelling. I never get over how much your mind can conjure up impending disaster. Then when you step into the light of day, in other words, step out of your mind, it's often shocking that everything's ticking along just fine. The sun is shining. People are busy. Smiling. Saying hello like life is great. Hey, didn't anyone hear those rocks last night? Wasn't anyone scared? Apparently not. Imagined doom?

There was nothing left to do, but the best thing possible. Walk to our favorite Telluride bakery and enjoy the ritual of croissant picking. "I'll have a chocolate one." "I'll take the cheese and ham." "Oh, maybe make it two." Sometimes, life is so easy. A hot cup of coffee, croissant in hand, people to chat with under the brilliant Colorado sun, was like breathing in the wonder of a new day, a new hike, a new stream to cool your feet, and the thought of a hot tub later.

Next? The always essential check-in at the Free Box (people drop off what they don't want and you find a treasure or someone fun to talk to).

By the time we got back to our site, the mystery was solved.

Right in front of us was the answer. The culprit of rock crashing noise? A 30-foot tree had fallen across our campsite. It was inches from the tent. The rock sounds in the night had been its preliminary cracking. There wasn't the slightest question about it...we could have died. We'd been warned. We were lucky.

I don't know why, but trees falling hadn't been something I had thought about. But yes, it happens. Something new to worry about.

Within hours, the saws were buzzing and our tree was removed. My perfect campsite—where a stream made this a prize location, offered bliss *and* a reality check.

You just never know what's going to happen. Could be something unfortunate. Like a falling tree. Or something good, like meeting someone in the campground bathroom who would change the course of your life for a few days. I couldn't resist sharing my tree story with the nice person I'd just met over a sink as we were brushing our teeth. "I'm here for the Telluride Mushroom Festival," she offered. "It starts tomorrow." I instantly knew I wanted to go. But how? After bonding over toothpaste, we opened the door to leave the bathroom and there was Travis talking to the organizer of the festival. He'd secured complimentary tickets for the four-day event in exchange for taking photographs. I got to go along!

Serendipity while brushing your teeth? Why not?

And what a ride! There we were, hiking through the woods, hunting for mushrooms, and sharing our treasures with Gary Lindcoff, famed mushroom expert and author of the *Audubon Guide to Mushrooms*. He was everything you'd hope a leader and teacher would be. If you brought him a shriveled up, common mushroom, he'd take it in his hands and examine it as though it was a precious jewel. He'd find something of value to share and at the same time light up confidence in a novice mushroom hunter, whose simple ordinary mushroom turned into a gift for all. I loved the message that "all things have value." There's always something interesting in the simple gifts of life.

The unexpected kept unfolding. Like marching in the mushroom parade? Not for me, thank you.

Hundreds of people dressed up in mushroom-themed costumes marching down Telluride's main street to mark the end of the festival was my next test. The question: would I join in? Walk in a parade? In a costume? This was something I'd never do. Or was it? How did I feel? Oh, yeah. "Come on Sandy. You don't know anyone here. Why are you so uptight?" I questioned myself. Was I brave enough to take a chance of looking kind of silly? Was I? Travis had already said a definite NO. Was I willing to go alone?

I was still pondering my decision (rarely a fast activity for me), as we wandered through some thrift shops and garage sales (always a favorite treasure hunt). And then I noticed a red and white polka dot scarf. For mushroom enthusiasts, the red and white dotted Amanita Muscaria (mushroom) is a favorite image. So was this a sign? "You have no excuse," I said to myself. A dollar later it was mine. A few minutes later it was tied around my head, and I was walking down the main street of Telluride chanting with everyone, "We love mushrooms!"

This was so NOT me. But it was so much FUN! I wouldn't have wanted to miss this. I was now a true participant in the festival. Since then, I've also found myself in other "put yourself out there and look silly" opportunities. The memory of being a mushroom chanter has pushed me to try that " I look like a fool" option. And oh, what I've missed by being self-conscious and wondering how I look.

Unexpected danger? Unexpected silliness? Serendipity brushing your teeth, or finding exactly what you need in a thrift shop? When you step *into* experience, rather than away, serendipity often appears!

You never know what's going to happen next. Serious danger? New friends? Silly fun? Living bravely moment to moment means staying open and not putting the brakes on experience. Consider that if everything happens as you expect it to, what fun is that? Life with no surprises?

And what's wrong with looking silly, anyway? Should serious fun and silliness be on my *Bravery Becomes You* list of essential steps? Absolutely.

GETTING BRAVER—WHAT I LEARNED ABOUT FEAR: *The unexpected happens all the time.*

That's the natural cycle of living. We all know the truth that "everything is always changing." And that's exactly what you want when you're ready to grow and create your unique vision of life.

Want to know the answer to "what's next?" You need the flow of experience. You need to keep going.

When our inner programming says, "Halt! Danger ahead!" or "That's silly," or even, "Don't do it; you'll regret it," we often stop. And then? We regret that we've missed out. We didn't grow. We didn't heed the truth, "If you don't change…nothing will change!"

Allowing experience room to happen, stepping away from thinking that something is good or bad, allows energy to flow. The best choice? Don't think. FEEL. Keep going.

That day in Telluride, I let intuition be my guide as well as my *Get Brave Compass*. I moved through each experience gathering information, learning, and growing without getting stuck on "why did that happen?" Everything that occurred became a part of my bravery experiment. The danger of almost dying under a fallen tree became a great tale of survival (and luck). The chance meeting in the bathroom led to an amazing education about mushrooms. Marching in the mushroom parade pushed me to be silly and vulnerable. And yet it turned out to be a favorite experience.

My biggest lesson? Don't let the NOs divert the flow of "what's next." Because in that stream of serendipitous energy may be wonderful gifts you didn't expect.

No question, the "over 50 and up phase of life" is all about the unexpected, which makes this the perfect time to test bravery, discover things about yourself you never knew, and become resilient and resourceful. The power to embrace change and not worry if you can handle it is yours to enjoy if you accept the challenge.

And no one has a story like yours. Your conflicts, successes, and failures are unique. There is no life history that doesn't include a full range of emotions: some you like and some don't. Some experiences are fair and others are not. The key is to embrace them. After all, you are the hero of your own adventure. You have the power to find peace, contentment, and enjoy a satisfying, meaningful future.

But can you change? Really? Now? Right now? Yes. Just do something different. Try out something that's missing.

Like fun. It's often the last thing on our lists, and yet it not only changes you but transforms the energy of the moment to joy which keeps expanding.

Practice change by having fun? Why not. It's a game-changer!

Your Turn

STOP #24

VIEW *from the*
SCENIC OVERLOOK

LOOKING OUT at your future, see yourself enjoying the energy of fun. What are you doing, or what would you like to do?

SHIFT GEARS: Make a fun date with yourself. How about today? It can be anything…big or small. What will you do?

EMERGENCY BRAKE: Fun? That's silly.

COMPASS CHECK-IN: Practice fun? or Don't want more fun.

Now consider: How do I feel if I do? How do I feel if I don't?

Yes? No? Is it a GO?

BRAVE TRAVEL TIP: Serendipity transforms the map of your future.

NEXT:
Saying NO

25

NO, NO, NO

Sweet Gratitude

I WAS GETTING USED TO FEAR, and liking it. I felt an excitement that I hadn't felt in a long time. It was a different kind of thrill. It was the joy of confidence. Trusting myself to do more than I had before. I was discovering things about myself that I imagined might be there, but I'd never seen evidence like this before. Action and evidence matter.

So there we were, hiking in Telluride. "I think I can't breathe," I offered as we scrambled over some rocks. The altitude was a consideration. But I had learned that when I felt uncomfortable and couldn't catch my breath, I just needed to take a break, drink some water, and within minutes keep going. It felt good to listen to myself and what I needed to do. I never felt that I was holding up the hike. Travis would sometimes go ahead (I encouraged him to do this), but he never went far and always waited for me.

We'd made it about halfway, and the trail began to take a different shape. The surface was tilting down toward a ravine far below. Gravity was not helping! "I don't think I can do this," I called out. Travis was ahead of me at that point but quickly came back. I held his arm while I maneuvered across the uncomfortable slant of trail. Relieved in one way, fearful in another, "I have to go back that way!" But for now, I was ready to keep going.

Things got worse. The ground kept sloping downward, except now the ground was covered with fine gravel and my shoes weren't gripping. There were no trees or branches to hold onto. "It's fine. Keep going," came the call from ahead. I tried. My feet slipped, and I started going toward the edge. This was an uphill climb, and I was going downhill. I tried again. Same result. Now I felt shaky. I had scared myself. "You go ahead. I'll wait here," I called back. He did and I found a nice rock to sit on. I waited. I did a short meditation and tried to stop thinking about sliding down the hill. I had worn the wrong shoes. Didn't anyone understand? No.

Soon, Travis returned with a story that a boulder had fallen and missed him by inches. "See! Good thing I hadn't gone." Now I had escaped a falling tree and a boulder tumbling down the mountain.

It was time to go back. Wouldn't that have been nice and easy! It wasn't for me. When we got to the slanted part of the trail that I'd maneuvered before, I couldn't do it. I had scared myself before, and fear wasn't letting go. It was probably ridiculous. But not to me. "I can't do it," was a firm "NO" from me. "You have to," was the answer. My body wouldn't budge. NO NO NO...kept shouting inside of me. "There's absolutely no way I'm doing this," I said. And now? Tears began to flow. (I haven't cried so many times in years, as on this trip, but bravery builds new skills!) So there I was crying. Firmly stating NO. I was surveying the ravine to see if there was some way to climb down the rocks. Impossible. Travis reached out to help me. "NO! I can't!" I confirmed with an edge of anger in my voice. Why had I ever said yes to this? I wanted to be brave. I felt helpless. But I felt a weird kind of strong, which showed up as another big NO! I also wondered, "What is wrong with me???" I had never felt so sure of anything, but it didn't feel good. I'd also never felt so firm about not letting anyone convince me that I was wrong. My inner voice said NO, and I was listening. Maybe this was the ultimate listening lesson. I've never heard myself so clearly.

Just when I thought everything was hopeless, a nice young couple and their dog came down from the top of the trail. They were the first people I'd seen the whole time we'd been there. They instantly saw my dilemma. "We can help you," they offered. "This isn't easy, and we totally understand." Accepting their kindness, I wrapped my arms with their arms on each side of me, and we inched, I mean inched...one inch by one inch by one inch, over the part of the trail that had scared me. I was crying the whole time.

"Thank you so much," I answered. "I don't know what I would have done without you." I added, "I'm not usually like this. I just couldn't do it." They were beyond nice. I was beyond weak. How could this be me?

Later I wondered how these people showed up out of nowhere? The perfect people at the perfect moment who transformed my "I can't do this" into instant trust. I felt safe with their help. I could see that this was a magic moment, even through the tears that were still flowing.

They were the heroes this time. And I was brave enough to say out loud, "I'm vulnerable. I'm embarrassed. I'm scared. I need your help," while crying on a mountaintop in the middle of paradise.

Bravery shows up in many ways.

Footnote: This wasn't a story I felt proud of at the time. But what's funny is this is one of my favorite stories. I was traumatized by the whole incident. Did I now have vertigo? It took other hikes and other risks to get over my fear. But strangely enough, there was something about being that scared and surviving that left me, once again, with a great story to tell. I was brave enough to try and fail. I said NO when I wanted to. I didn't let this alter my enthusiasm for whatever would come next (I faced another uncomfortable walk, but did it anyway.) I was brave enough to try again. And I'd also felt the serene joy of having strangers care enough to take the time to help and be so nice about it.

Wherever they are. Thank you.

GETTING BRAVER—WHAT I LEARNED ABOUT FEAR: *I'm grateful for fear.*

Fear has awakened my emotional intelligence and the awareness to listen to myself for direction. Fear has given me the power to say yes or no and feel empowered by my choice. Fear may be the opposite of how I want to feel, but it's warnings are both an alert to be careful (which is important) and to also be true to myself. There's no better signal to remind me that I don't want to automatically choose what's comfortable. And lastly, transcending fear shows me the strength I have to stay focused on my vision of the future.

Now fear feels good. It may seem strange, but that edge of uncomfortable is an opportunity. I know that if I take a step, there's great satisfaction on the other side of that action. Crossing to the other side means I'm stronger than I thought. Even better, the more I do that, the stronger I become. I'm grateful for that!

One of the most joyful awakenings of this trip was the power of gratitude to add meaning and satisfaction to every moment, whether fearful or fear-free. Having the chance to experience that endless supply of good feelings made my heart full, 24 hours a day.

We often think of being grateful for what we like and what's good. But now I'm also adding fear to that list. I learned a lot that day.

How about you? Can you see how fear is something to put on your gratitude list?

Note: When fear means physical danger, NO is always the answer I choose. I'm grateful for the warning.

Your Turn

STOP #25

VIEW *from the* SCENIC OVERLOOK

LOOKING OUT at your precious future, can you be grateful for what fear has shown you about you? Were you able to accept that you were afraid and honor that? Write it down.

SHIFT GEARS: Have you been proud about how you handled fear? Did it make you stronger?

EMERGENCY BRAKE: Fear scares me. I'm not grateful for that.

COMPASS CHECK-IN: Gratitude and growth from fear? or Disappointment?

Now consider: How do I feel if I do? How do I feel if I don't?

Yes? No? Is it a GO?

BRAVE TRAVEL TIP: Fear creates the opportunity to be grateful over and over again.

NEXT:
Road of Tears

26

Fear of Falling

Brave Self-Care to the Rescue

ALL I COULD THINK OF WERE WILDFLOWERS. I'd heard, over and over again on this trip, that Crested Butte was a magical destination. We still had mushrooms on our minds, but....you know...things change. Now I just had to see wildflowers.

What I got was a road of tears. This time we weren't waiting until dark to find our campsite. We were on our way, heading UP again. Like so many roads this one was the same - a narrower and narrower, drop-off-the-side style of road. It curved. Went up. Curved. Up. Narrower. UP. Rocky. UP. I was beyond scared, again. I had no reason not to be. Good instincts! I later found out that cars had gone over the side. I didn't like this. And this was a two-way road that wasn't. Erosion had made it very narrow! Again! A car coming the other way. Someone's got to back up on the curving, steep, single lane. Oh, joy. I kept hoping it wouldn't be us.

I could see clearly what was ahead. Where we were, the road was full of rocks of various sizes. The wheels were often churning against the rubble while rocking side to side. The edge was close. This didn't feel good.

So I tried my compass:

How do I feel if I do? How do I feel if I don't?

Through my tears, I was getting better at listening to myself. I was getting better at knowing what was acceptable to me. I didn't care what anyone thought. "I'm getting out." That was my answer. My "I don't" was firm. My "I do"? "I'll meet you at the top."

And I got out. Travis kept going. "Was I going to let my child go over the edge? And what would I do if he did?" A no control moment was just that. It was what it was.

I could hear the car rev its engine to get over the rocks. I watched it rock and tip. I walked behind. This was a slow process. It was easy to keep up.

I was still shaking a bit from the drive so far, but I no longer had to be afraid (at least for me). It felt good. I'd stood up for what I thought was best. I knew clearly that I'm not responsible for other people's choices, whether I like them or not.

My fear barometer was working. I didn't listen to the voices in my head: "You sound like the mom," and "You aren't a very strong outdoor person," and "You're out of your element" (what's that anyway?), and "Everyone else is doing this." Nope, this wasn't for me.

Travis got to the top of the road. I met him there. I got back in the car. All was well. He was fine with my choice.

We found our site and later hiked up part of the trail at Schofield Pass that was nearby. I could feel the altitude in my breathless steps, but I'd gotten used to that. I just had to go slower, rest, and drink water. I couldn't wish it away. We hiked through the woods. Mushrooms everywhere. Surround sound—silence. An occasional snap of a branch. And then the views! Vast. This is a well-known path, where hikers trek from Crested Butte to Aspen. The Maroon Bells (mountains) towered in the distance. And wildflowers, wilting at the end of their season, were, yes...magical. It didn't matter that the season of full-bloom was over. I didn't care.

I could still imagine their former beauty. Their presence, while faded, was everywhere. The scene was fairytale majestic. And of course, getting lost is part of most fairytale stories, which meant we did lose our way and found ourselves walking in mud and water, my sneakers drenched and squishy as we walked...and walked...and walked. I'd say we were on the brink of "I hope we're going the right direction," when we passed another hiker who said, "You're brave to be on this path." Perfect. I loved it. My word. My fearless skills acknowledged.

We made some lucky turns and found our way back to the opening of the path. Tired and wet, we still had to hike back to our campsite, but as it so often happened on our trip, people offered us a ride! We needed it.

Serendipity on the trail. The camaraderie, sharing information, tips, ideas, and favorite places made conversation lively. We weren't just feeling connected to nature. We were connected to people too.

GETTING BRAVER—WHAT I LEARNED ABOUT FEAR: *Fear is the mother of nurturing.*

Taking care of the hurt and loss of confidence that fear creates is the hallmark of empathy and understanding that life is scary! But what if you turn the tables and feel sorry for fear. Poor fear, trying so hard to keep you safe from harm (which is valid, thank you). Sadly fear misunderstands that discomfort encourages personal growth. What's scary is not growing!

Bravery is the ultimate resource for taking care of you. You can stand up for what's best for you, and you know it. If you activate your brave intelligence and feel the vibrant joy of your confidence, you not only feel motivated, energized, and focused, you've elevated your "vibe" to the bliss of being there for you, no matter what. And once you know that, it's easy to ask fear to move aside.

So when I got out of the car and walked, I was practicing self-care. It felt good.

And that's why solving conflict is so much easier when *Bravery Becomes You*. Once you understand the power of brave confidence, fear sits in the back seat. You are a blissful driver!

What about you? Are you a good caregiver of your future?

Your Turn

STOP #26

VIEW *from the*
SCENIC OVERLOOK

IT'S TIME to drive in reverse! Imagine the future has arrived. Who you always longed to be, happened! Now look back in time. See the strength it took to keep yourself a #1 priority. How did it feel to honor yourself?

SHIFT GEARS: Now see how you nurtured yourself and took care of that seed of potential, yearning to grow. What did you do?

EMERGENCY BRAKE: I can't trust that I'll be that persistent.

COMPASS CHECK-IN: Believe you can nurture who you want to be? or Forget it.

Now consider: How do I feel if I do? How do I feel if I don't?

Yes? No? Is it a GO?

BRAVE TRAVEL TIP: Nurturing dreams is essential self-care.

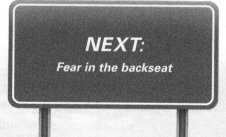

NEXT:
Fear in the backseat

27

Entering the Brave Zone

An End is a Beginning

CRESTED BUTTE WAS NOT THE END. It was a turning point. I had been brave so many times that bravery had become part of who I was. I was getting used to thinking with an open mind that was curious rather than judgmental. Feeling exuberant was the norm.

Now I was constantly having aha moments where I felt like shouting out the windows of the car, "What was I worried about anyway?" I sure have spent a lot of my life worrying about a whole lot of nothing.

We still had weeks and endless miles to go. Experience was waiting to unfold. My list of stories of empowerment had grown. I couldn't wait to share them with everyone.

Our journey continued as we drove through Nevada on Route 50, "The Loneliest Road in America." The area is home to countless UFO stories (there have been over 100 sightings). I considered them as we slept in the middle of nowhere under a pale pink light, glowing in the distance. Were we really driving past signs that said, "Extraterrestrial Highway?" Stopping at the A'Le'Inn (pronounced "alien") for coffee, and the Alien Research Center (a souvenir store), was unexpected fun.

During the six weeks of driving and exploring with my son, my focus never swayed from becoming brave. It was a test for a confessed scaredy-cat. ME. And throughout all the wonder, bravery didn't disappoint. It was my guide, my guru, and my greatest trusted ally as we went wherever curiosity led.

"No rules" travel gave us a favorite term…Loopin! Drive back to where we'd just been because there was something we missed? Of course! That wouldn't have made sense to "pre-trip" me, but now it was normal. Why would you want to miss anything if it were easily doable? You wouldn't!

Fear had been steering my life. Why worry about what change could do to me? Is there something I'd lose by changing?

Now I knew that what I want to hold onto or let go of is my choice. And without question, there's a lot to let go of. Like…things I don't want. Goals and dreams that no longer resonate. Outcomes that I don't care about at all. I'd been fooling myself for years. I had been repeating patterns of behavior that didn't make me feel good. The truth? There's nothing to lose but what you don't want. There's nothing to gain but what you desire. I want that!

The idea of living fearless and free energized my future. It showed me that being brave is the outcome I want, whatever happens. Every experience is a lesson. A reason to grow. A chance to thrive.

As we headed back to Boulder to spend a few days with family, I was thrilled to have a new kind of story to share. The tale I told wasn't based on where I went. It was about who I used to be and who I'd become.

I had entered the brave zone. I liked it here. It was comfortable!

GETTING BRAVER FOR THE REST OF MY LIFE!—*What I learned about fear: Fear is along for the ride.*

It will always be with me. It's an essential part of my journey.

But it's not what I thought it was. It has its time and place.

How about you? Want to join me at my last stop? The brave zone!

Here's my new truth: Everyone, including me, talks about the dreaded comfort zone. It's a mythological place where we retreat, thinking that we're taking care and protecting ourselves from discomfort. Not true! I now see that the traditional comfort zone is the most uncomfortable place I've ever been. But the good news?

Welcome to the brave zone, the self-care capital, where true comfort resides. And *Bravery Becomes You* is a direct route to this lovely place where it feels good to push yourself that extra bit, and accept new challenges. Here, uncomfortable is actually comfortable. It's a sign of positive change.

The brave zone creates strong, protective boundaries around what you want to do and how you want to live. You discover that you don't need to lose yourself in the shuffle of daily routines and old patterns of behavior. You don't ever forget who you are.

It's a safe place where bravery is your 24-hour-a-day guide.

Now, I wake up every day with clear direction and joy because my focus for the future is simply to be brave. That's it. And since it's safe here, I can try the future on for size. Get rid of what no longer fits and wear my new self with style and grace. What fun!

And it doesn't matter if I know what's next. I just know how I want to feel. I want to say I DO more than I DON'T.

When I turn on brave thinking, then no matter what I choose to do is always in my best interest. Self-care to the rescue! I can be comfortable being fearless and free...my way. How about you? How does being brave and comfortable sound?

Your Turn

VIEW from the
SCENIC OVERLOOK

AS YOU stand at the overlook, consider how you would like your future story to read.

As Future You, what would you like to tell your family, friends, and community about how you took the risk to honor what was important to you and moved forward with brave intent.

Will your story be that you were brave enough to try no matter what? Imagine what you would say. What stopped you? What didn't? Why did you never give up? Use your imagination. Pretend. Have fun. Be creative. Be wild!

SHIFT GEARS: Imagine that you're sage with wisdom and a powerful story— a gift to share. Everyone wants to believe that they can also let go of what holds them back and embrace the joy of living life with meaning and purpose. You are an inspiration. Your story can make a difference in other people's lives. You believed in yourself. Now, you are spreading hope with your experience. How would you like to inspire others?

EMERGENCY BRAKE: I never tried. I was afraid of change.

COMPASS CHECK-IN: Take a chance, create the story of your future or head to the comfort zone, put your feet up and do nothing.

Now consider: How do I feel if I do? How do I feel if I don't?

Yes? No? Is it a GO?

BRAVE TRAVEL TIP: Bring on the fear, the discomfort, and the adventure of the unknown.

PART III

Unpacking Bravery

28

The Habit of Bravery

Unpacking Bliss Every Day

I'M HOME. Me. Happy. Satisfied. Content. Confident. Scared? Yes. Still scared. Still worrying.

Does transformation last? What makes it stick?

I could feel it. That old habit of not trusting that a happy, healthy mindset will last was hovering nearby. Overwhelm, day-to-day details, responsibility, drudgery, and the monotony of my procrastination were asking the same old question, "Will this time be different?" I could hear the voices of the NOs, chomping at the bit to teach me a lesson. Who, you? Brave? Camping? Big deal.

Yes, ME! That's who. Me—the one who was ready to live in the brave zone. Because now I know the truth. Bravery means stepping up to be the hero of my own self-care. I'd discovered the joy of CARING ABOUT ME!!! And that means looking out for my dreams, my health, my work, my clients, and my future. It means nurturing and standing up for what feels good and right, for what's empowering, and soul-fulfilling. It was time to make that promise. Cross my heart! But that nagging fear was still asking? Will you?

This time, yes. Bravery felt so good. I owed it to myself to keep going.

So when the vacation glow softened, the phone started ringing, the work started flowing, the laundry started growing, and "what's for dinner?" was on repeat. I knew I'd be okay.

Bravery was now my belief system, my self-care routine, my source of energy, and confidence. I could be uncomfortable with change and know that a small amount of uneasiness was the price of the fearless freedom I wanted. I had fully entered the brave zone.

I knew I'd be unpacking the lessons of my trip for a while and the first "note to self" out of my suitcase was, "I am making PERSISTENT, RESILIENT, SERIOUS, *BRAVERY BECOMES YOU* SELF-CARE a non-negotiable priority for the rest of my life."

This new attitude would take work, awareness, intention, and more inner reflection. And since I know from my history that it's easy to forget all of this, I knew I needed to keep brave me awake by setting clear boundaries around my dreams, both to keep them safe from distraction and to manage time for other important things—like work, fun, health, relationships, money, and even my own attitude. Clarity was also asking that big "what's next?" question. But now, it wasn't a threat and even if I didn't know what to do, I knew I could trust how I wanted to feel. I had a compass! Indecision solved!

Digging further into the contents of my bag, I also unpacked an emblem of my new brave identity. Oh, joy! My favorite! The lavender bandana that I'd worn every day on the trip...a treasure I'd found at the prep stage of "getting ready," back at that Goodwill store in Eugene, Oregon.

I loved the look of this new me that I knew would unfold and unwrinkle with time. (Well, not in all ways...darn!)

Waking up in the morning would start with brave intentions and clarity. I could relax knowing that whatever came my way would be manageable because of my brave lens of confidence. It was easier to push aside the pointless worry that always got in my way before. I had also become a persistent advocate for letting go of outdated patterns of thinking while opening the door to undiscovered territory. It was inspiring to believe that change is possible!

My trusty *Get Brave Compass* would also help me feel my way through each day. I could ask, "How do I feel if I do? How do I feel if I don't?" no matter the size of the question. I was overjoyed to find it was just as effective back home. I tried it out on something small first—dinner. The choice? Cook a meal from scratch (which I didn't feel like doing at the moment) or choose an easy premade and delicious option? And so I asked my question. I took a moment to feel my choices. I saw myself serving dinner both ways. The answer? Cook from scratch. It would make the evening special. I liked that. And that's what I did. And all of a sudden I had energy I didn't have before. What had seemed a chore moments before instantly became fun.

Life is so much easier when you know what you want. And if you don't know, ask!!!

Most of all, a brave identity makes all things possible. Inner guidance and intuition offer creative solutions, compassionate problem solving, and loving self-care that looks out for your best interests all the time.

So what will you do with so much inner support, power, and wisdom? How will you define success? Have fun? Is it possible to simply enjoy who you are? Brave you says YES.

But one more question…

How do you keep your brave identity fearless and free?

Oh, yeah. Here it comes. The #1 solution to handling that big interfering army of NOs.

NEXT:
Can bravery and fear get along?

29

Give Fear a Job

Meet Your 24-Hour-a-Day Personal Assistant

THE TRUTH IS THAT FEAR has good intentions. It wants to keep you safe and comfortable. So if you give it practical, organizational tasks focused on what you want to do, then you've discovered a superpower support system. Keeping fear busy and relaxed will reduce the NOs it might otherwise toss your way.

Some suggestions that will make fear feel comfortable. Set your alarm to remind you that it's time to take a walk. Or meditate. Or take a step toward the vision that you've been creating throughout this book.

Silence your phone notifications and consider how you're talking to yourself. Is your inner voice supportive or negative? The NOs might be talking!

Write down your steps/goals in a calendar. It makes them real! You've got a date to take action.

Want to have more fun? Let fear order tickets for a concert, or check out what's happening where you live.

And if you want some help with action steps, ask fear to order library books, or call an expert who can help you. Research on the computer.

Have fear leave you reminder notes like Remember The Brave Zone! or Drink More Water.

Fear's control will relax if it believes that risks are small and manageable.

When you have a new idea, take small steps. It will give fear a chance to get comfortable with change.

Once you give fear enough to do, it will believe (because it's true) that everything is okay. Structure calms fear by providing comfort, and when it's comforted, it doesn't get activated (as much). The battle within to stay the same or grow will soften with time.

So, now that fear has a job, it's time for the adventure of YOU. Fearless and free. Nurtured and supported. Content and confident as you let go of the past and create your future with energy and the power of joy.

As I liked to say on our journey...It's time to put your dreams in the driver's seat, toss fear in the back, and head off into your best life. As always, your way. With your brave self flying free.

30

Beginnings

One year later...

WHAT HAPPENED WHEN BRAVERY BECAME ME? I found myself hungry for change and adventure. I welcomed fear as a sign that something was about to happen. I pushed myself to take action (despite my fears) because, more than anything, I wanted to say yes to who I wanted to be and how I wanted to live. Bravery had become a habit that supercharged my confidence with the energy to do what I said I wanted to do. What a relief!!!

Yes, something was different, and it lasted beyond the glow of my trip. My life changed and so did my coaching business that's now thriving with the life-transforming message of bravery. I love working with my clients more than ever. They appreciate the empowering, practical wisdom of the *Bravery Becomes You* mindset that leads to satisfied living. Overcoming fear and embracing bravery can create the future they want. All dreams are possible! That was my story, and now it is theirs too. The power of bravery activates joyful and meaningful change for everyone.

My *Get Brave Compass* has also become everyone's #1 favorite life-changing tool. Following the guidance of emotions and intuition, checking out the pros and cons by imagining and feeling possible outcomes, works! All that struggle about what to do? It's there one minute and gone the next. Action replaces doubt and increases the fearless energy of confidence.

In an instant, you're moving forward with the joy of what you want to feel. You're on the way to a future based on what you *really* want.

Remember the "old" way of thinking first, which means checking in with the past to figure out the future? There's no faster way to put the brakes on "what's next." Now you know a better way to make decisions. Feel first!!!

And adventures? The fun continues for me. An 11-hour flight to Hawaii with no hotel and no itinerary? Why not? A trip to Canada that included a familiar worry, "We're driving how far?" Yes! But when I accepted the outrageous route we were taking, I was able to sit back and enjoy every minute (camping included!).

Today, what's most important to me is how much I enjoy sharing what I learned from living my bravery experiment. This book was the result of loving an idea that needed an action plan. I was stuck knowing that *Bravery Becomes You* was a great concept. But what to do? I got the message loud and clear that an idea isn't enough. It needs activation, curiosity, and the insight of imagination to grow beyond the seed of thought.

My belief is that we all have something we're longing to do and for many reasons we get stuck not knowing how to begin. I hope my journey inspires you to jump-start yours. The understanding that you don't have to know where you're going, you just have to know how you want to feel and be brave enough to begin, is all you need to live fearless and free.

And so my challenge to you...

What would you do if you were brave? What step will you take? One more time?

HOW WILL I FEEL IF I DO? HOW WILL I FEEL IF I DON'T?

And now that we've traveled so far together, let's keep going. Brave, Fearless, and Free. There's no better way to be!

(See the last page of the book for more information.)

And now? A word from Travis...

The View According to Travis

MY SKI SEASON, LIVING IN Telluride working as a "lifty," had just ended. I got in my car and headed to Utah to go on a rafting trip. This is where my nonstop journey across the American West began and eventually continued later with my mom. This wasn't just a road trip, it was the experience of freely, spontaneously traveling with no real plans or expectations; going with the flow to see what serendipitous moments would unfold, encompassed by the everlasting wonders of nature.

With a tent, my Subaru, and USA Atlas I directed my drive by what looked like the coolest next place to experience, even if it meant going out of the way (which is often the right way).

I was heading west on route 50 through Nevada, also known as the loneliest highway in the USA. With no radio signal and the same Grateful Dead CDs on repeat, I had a lot of time to think. I realized that this journey of living, immersed in nature with a tent, camping in national parks, swimming in rivers and oceans, and driving on scenic roads, needed to be shared.

And so I called my mom when I got service and asked if she wanted to fly out west and join in on this journey. I knew that my curiosity was about to get the best of me and I wanted her to see what was about to happen. I had been to some amazing places, but I knew that once I made it further west it was only going to get more beautiful. The anticipation of making it out to Oregon and Washington to see the glaciers, rainforests, and coast-lines gave me the feeling that I had gone too far to turn back.

So I told my mom to book a plane ticket to Portland and join me for the best part of this road trip. I could tell she was hesitant, but also in-trigued by the idea. It seemed like she was saying no, but deep down she was curious. My mom had never camped before, but I knew if she got out of her comfort zone and let bravery become her that she would appreciate sleeping under the stars in a tent.

My mom was back and forth about going, unsure if she was ready for a completely unplanned trip with no itinerary, camping in a tent, traveling in unfamiliar territory.

It was the moment when she was getting her haircut and her stylist told her that it would be crazy not to go, that her answer changed. With new encouragement and a sense of bravery, she said yes.

Our journey had now begun and I knew we were off for an adventure.

My mom started her trip by almost getting on a flight to Portland, Maine instead of Portland, Oregon. Nonetheless, she finally arrived.

When she got to the airport, I picked her up and we immediately went against what she thought the plan might have been, which ended up being a theme for the rest of the trip. Instead of going straight to see her cousins in Eugene, Oregon we went to a trendy food truck eatery you only see in Portland. I knew it was worth going out of our way and that it was some-thing we shouldn't miss. My mom would come to realize why. As the trip went along we had many instances like this, such as turning what for most people would be a three-day drive into a single 11-hour adventure through the Trinity Alps. We were headed to a small town to see a band I knew was worth seeing live. I had heard this band before at the Oregon Country Fair and it was a musical performance my mom had to experience. She was brave enough to go with the flow and I think she'd say that going out of our way was worth it. She also realized what happens when you let the journey become the destination.

As the trip went along I was enjoying sharing this serendipitous, go with the flow lifestyle, as I searched for the wonders of nature with my mom. I appreciated seeing what was new as well as showing her places I had been before that were special to me.

I had been to Mammoth for skiing in July, tubed the Merced River through Yosemite, and experienced the tallest mountain in the country, Mt. Whitney. I made sure we went out of our way to see these places on the southern loop of our trip.

My mom was brave and was always up for what the day had in store. I was able to share the experience of having no real plan while enjoying every moment as much as where we were going. *Bravery Becomes You* when you get on the road without worrying where it may lead you. You learn to enjoy the magic that appears along the way.

During our trip, we made it to Yosemite where we stayed in a secret camping spot I knew about from talking to locals and we swam in the frigid cold water of Fish Camp. My mom was hesitant at first but then got in the water. I could tell that she was happy and refreshed and finally got that shower she had wanted after days without one. After learning how amazing this fresh natural river water felt I could see her embracing future swimming spots and the nature around her.

On our first night camping on the beach in Oregon, she seems frightened by the thought of sleeping on a random beach. I got the tent set up and made it comfortable. In the morning when we woke up to our waterfront property I think she was seeing what is so special about camping.

Over time my mom went from being scared to being brave and excited about the next place to camp or swim. For example, when we got to Zion to hike the Narrows we discovered there was a flash flood warning. All the conditions were pointing to not going on the hike. Earlier on the trip my mom would have said no, but now she knew that since we had come all this way, we should at least give it a try. We got around a few bends of the slot canyon but realized it was too dangerous to continue. Even though our hike was shortened, the experience was still great. At this point, she was going with the flow. Bravery had become her and she was able to experience the calmness and serenity of nature.

By the end of our six-week road trip, she had camped countless nights, taken "showers" in many rivers, adventured through Oregon, Washington, California, Nevada, Utah, and Colorado, and been to dozens of National Parks.

Traveling from Eugene south six hours out of our way, to swim in one of the clearest rivers in California (the Smith River), then back up north along the Oregon Washington coast through the rainforests and over the Olympic mountains, across the sound from Bainbridge to Seattle, north to Mount Baker and across the Cascade Mountain range to Chelan and Stehekin, down and around Mount Rainier, into the crater of Mount Saint Helens, back to Eugene, down the California coast to San Francisco, Santa Barbara and Venice Beach in L.A. was just part one of our trip.

From highway 1 to the 101 to the 5 to the 405 and back into nature we continued to see the largest trees in the world in Sequoia National Park, the glacial carved valley of Yosemite, and crossed the Sierra Nevada mountains on our way to Mammoth. We then went from the tallest mountain in the United States, Mount Whitney, to the lowest point in the country, Death Valley. From Death Valley, we made our way through "alien" country in Nevada and into the Grand Escalante staircase of Utah. We went from the narrows in Zion, to the hoodoos in Bryce Canyon to the fossilized sea floor of Capitol Reef.

We made our way around the country with no plan, seeing all the most amazing things nature had to offer, allowing the adventure to unfold along the way.

The rest of the trip was daily serendipity. No rules, a vague itinerary that could change moment by moment, and beautiful weather gave us a good start. I was happy to share the way I like to travel. When you get on the road without worrying where it may take you, every moment is as fun and exciting as arriving at whatever destination was "sort of" planned.

We've traveled together since then, and I'm sure we will again. Our trip was a great memory for both of us and I was glad to be part of my Mom's *Bravery Becomes You* experiment. I think she found out that when you "get over" being scared, you discover the confidence to say yes to the next adventure, and the next. That's how I like to live my life, and I believe that now she wants that too.

Three Brave Tools:

1

A View from the Scenic Overlook:
CREATING A GET BRAVE MAP

WOULDN'T IT BE NICE TO SEE the coming attractions of your future story? Or try out the future before you get there? Time to create your own unique "inner map" that will guide you to a future that's aligned with YOU.

The *Get Brave Map* takes form every time you arrive at *View from the Scenic Overlook,* at the end of each chapter. It's here that you use your imagination and picture a future that appeals to you.

By envisioning who you want to be, you're creating a powerful reference map of your desired life. And the more you do this, the easier it becomes to let go of the old map of your past and follow a vibrant new path to the future! The *Get Brave Map* will remember where you want to go and guide you there.

It works like this:

See the future you desire. (You can do this by imagining a movie theater in your mind that shows you a place where all possibility exists).

Now activate that vision by adding the magic ingredient...Feel it like you're *really* there. See that *view*, then let your senses come alive. Be there. Are there sounds, smells, tastes? Notice every detail (colors, clouds, birds singing, music playing). See and feel who you *really* want to be and how you want to live. How does that feel?

This is your chance to try on anything. Be anything. See if what you experience resonates with meaning, purpose, and passion. What fits? You may also try on things that you thought you wanted but once you experience them in your imagined future reality, they aren't a match. Be grateful for that time-saving discovery. Let them go.

Remember, this is a judgment-free test run. No rules. No right answers. This is an adventure of joy and pleasure as you take a moment to visit with Future You. Dream big. Dream anything you want. Go for it! Enjoy feeling inspired. You may find yourself smiling!

Here's a sample journey: Imagine a beautiful day somewhere in the future. You are the version of yourself you believed you could be. Allow the vision to flow. Enjoy it. Take it all in. What are you wearing? Are you alone? Happy? Content? Satisfied? Let your sensations run free. And then, the most important action? Embrace your future story like it's *actually* happening. You are there!

Bravery Bonus: Science says that your body doesn't know the difference between what's real and what's imagined when you make the future feel like you're *really* there. Your body believes it's had the experience. That's why the *Get Brave Map* is so powerful; it's a highly effective way of making change easier in the present. Your mind and body are primed to feel comfortable, confident, and brave. Obstacles lose their power. You don't.

The more you see your "future self" feeling the joy of being true to yourself, the more you will begin to notice that your steps flow with new comfort and ease. Solutions show up. Opportunities arrive. The reason? You've practiced. And as *Bravery Becomes You*, inspired confidence will energize your journey forward guided by your own personal *Get Brave Map*.

Whenever you arrive at *View from the Scenic Overlook* you know it's time to stop for a moment and imagine your future like it's *really* happening!

2

The Get Brave Compass

EVERY INNER JOURNEY NEEDS a *Get Brave Compass* that follows the north star of your true self. It's the 100% reliable GPS that answers the questions: What's the best choice at the moment?, as well as, What's next?, What's missing?, and Why don't I do what I say I want to do?

Indecision solved.

The following sentence will guide you in the perfect direction every time: HOW DO I FEEL IF I DO? HOW DO I FEEL IF I DON'T?

The *Get Brave Compass* is the ultimate decision-maker that guides you with instant clarity. When your busy mind is overthinking, worrying, and trying to make sense of everything that's happening, it can freeze with indecision. Clear direction equals brave confidence and action.

The *Get Brave Compass* works because it changes the auto-pilot response of your actions. So instead of choosing to act the way you always do, (like saying an automatic NO to what's not comfortable), YOU STOP and bring your attention directly to the question you want your compass to answer. You're now focused. Alert. Now, your own innate and reliable guidance comes through loud and clear. There's no better way to push past fear.

So let's say you have a dream of waterskiing. You want to say YES. But you also hear a big NO that says, "It's too late, you're too old, it's too hard, and you don't have skis." And you listen. Now use your compass. Imagine skiing. It feels amazing. You love that feeling. But what if you say NO. Do you *really* want to do that? How does that feel?

To make the decision that's right for you ask, "How do I feel if I do? (see yourself waterskiing) How do I feel if I don't? (see the big NO)." YES. NO. YES. NO. Is it a GO?

3

A Pen and a Journal

TO MAKE YOUR ADVENTURE MEMORABLE, fun, and effective you need something to write with. This book is not only about embracing brave change but also about making change last. Responding to the questions that follow each story by *thinking* the answers is fine but writing down the answers is best. Your participation and written words imprint your ideas and emotions in a way that gives them staying power. Your subconscious may have some interesting messages for you!

It works like this:

After each story that I share, you'll see, **VIEW FROM THE SCENIC OVERLOOK,** followed by questions and statements where you can pause, reflect, and consider how you would respond to fear, what you would learn, and what you would do if you were brave.

I suggest you create a journal for the adventure. Make it your own personal inner travel log!

Please remember to pack your humor, your imagination, and some fun along for the ride! Questions will guide you. I always suggest closing your eyes and taking a few calm breaths before you write your answers. Just let the words flow. Don't think too much!

Have fun. Enjoy the place where fear and bravery meet and learn how to get along.

A Special Thank You

THANK YOU TO MY SON, Travis, for being my extraordinary guide on our six-week camping road trip.

Your idea to go camping with me, your mother, who had never camped in her life, was a kind and generous gesture. This trip was so much more than a summer getaway. It was not only one of the great adventures of my life, it was an amazing opportunity to experience *Bravery Becomes You*, my philosophy about living life with passion, purpose, and joy.

Because of this journey, I lived with brave intention. I became my own action hero! Little did I know when we began, that I would test my fears, redefine vulnerability, let go of control and release resistance while living the reality that *Bravery Becomes You* is a practical, energizing, in the moment mindset, that makes standing up for who you are and how you want to live 100 percent possible. Bravery is about the joy of being alive!

My deepest appreciation and gratitude to Travis for making my dreams come true.

IN GRATITUDE AND APPRECIATION

I owe a debt of gratitude to the many friends and family who supported me through the very exciting yet often difficult process of writing this book. To ensure that the inner journey of awakening true bravery was authentic, I may have driven everyone a little crazy! Sifting through "the fluff" of positive thinking was a journey I couldn't have done alone.

To my husband John, who was such an important part of this road trip adventure, thank you for the many hours spent brainstorming creative solutions and words for the book as well as your patience and support despite my time-consuming relationship with my computer. To my daughter Katy and son Travis, who listened to my endless questions and constant requests for their opinions, I appreciate your kindness. Being with you both is my favorite adventure. Thank you all for being there for me. I'm sure it's not easy having a writer in the house!

A big thank you goes to Jan Case who was by my side from the start. Reading, editing, critiquing, and helping me sort through my thoughts while cheering me on when I had doubts was invaluable. You shared endless hours of time as well as your supreme analytical skills, ensuring the meaning and flow of the manuscript. I don't think this book would have happened without you. Thank you for being an amazing friend and for all the laughter that made this journey a delight!

To Sherry Rogers: I will always cherish our enviable "working vacations" where a lot of this book developed. You're not only a great and supportive friend, but someone who was always available to hear my concerns and successes. I could always ask, "Would you mind reading my book," again! Your patient nurturing, wisdom, and advice were essential to this book. I am so grateful for all you do.

MY SINCERE APPRECIATION ALSO GOES TO:

Nancy Schiller, great friend, and outstanding coach who kept me on track with good advice and lots of love and support.

Joan Heim, who not only offered encouragement, but is a sister I can always turn to for guidance, and friendship.

Diane Pawlowicz, who read, edited, cheered me on, and offered invaluable advice. Your friendship means a lot to me.

Paulette Forbes, a friend who not only read the book but added editing to the gift of her time. I am grateful for your input and careful attention to the manuscript.

Sydney Petty, reader, and friend. Thank you for always being there.

Jan Hudson, who shared insights, support, and valuable conversation. I appreciate all you do.

Shelley Rowe, whose words, "I can see *Bravery Becomes You* on the cover of a book," was the jump-start I needed to start writing.

Roxanne Farias Walsh who inspired me to say YES.

My cousins Chris and Charles Ogle who made this adventure extra special. Being with you was one of the best parts of the trip.

Gretchen Matthews, excellent editor, who also offered valuable support and feedback.

Many thanks for the friendship and advice of Louise White, Sarah Conway, Amanda Fegley, The Woos (Women of One), my book group, and all my family and friends. You are amazing!

Also, thanks to Peri Gabriel, award-winning book designer, whose talent brought this book's adventure to life.

In appreciation of Iris Krasnow, Shelley Rowe, Liz Fletcher Brown, Karin Sokel, and Gillian Stevens, for their generous praise of the book.

Special thanks to everyone at the Johns Hopkins Spiritual Practices Study, who supported an extraordinary journey of personal discovery that changed my life.

Writing this book was one of my biggest *Bravery Becomes You* adventures. I couldn't have done it without "my team" of friends and family.

✿

About the Author

SANDY TRAVIS BILDAHL is an award-winning writer, certified Emotional Intelligence and Business Coach, Inspirational Speaker, and Workshop Creator.

She believes that when *Bravery Becomes You*, internal struggles that are not aligned with your true self are released and replaced with the joy of feeling alive, satisfied and content. Awakening your own unique inner compass makes direction to the future clear and reveals a life you love.

The power of stories to create life-transforming change and deep connections with others has been the author's passion throughout her 30-year entrepreneurial career. She is also an artist whose art can be seen in shows and galleries.

This is her 4th book.

She loves the wonder of adventure, being scared, and living brave.

KEEP GOING! DON'T STOP NOW and let the happiness you want pass you by. There's so much joy waiting to be experienced. It's time to live a life you love and be YOU!

Your journey with Sandy doesn't have to end here. She hopes you'll stay in touch. There are several ways to do that.

COACHING WITH SANDY (still by your side)!

CONNECT WITH SANDY to learn more about her *Brave Coaching for Confidence, Contentment, and Courage* packages and programs by email: braverybecomesyou@gmail.com or on her website: www.braverybecomesyou.com.

SANDY IS ALSO AVAILABLE for speaking engagements, conferences, and workshops.

Bravery Becomes You online courses are also available. Send Sandy an email, and when enrollment opens, you will be contacted.

Bravery Becomes You: On the Road to Fearless and Free is available on Amazon or from the publisher, Worthwords Publishing.

Worthwords Publishing
www.worthwordspublishing.com

Made in United States
North Haven, CT
06 November 2021